FLOYD CLYMER'S MOTORCYCLIST'S LIBRARY

The Book of the
BSA TWINS

A Practical Guide to handling and maintenance for owners of all 500 and 650 cc O.H.V. Vertical Twins (A7 and A10) from 1948 to 1962 except 1962 models A50 and A65

W. C. Haycraft, F.R.S.A.

ANNOUNCEMENT

By special arrangement with the original publishers of this book, Sir Isaac Pitman & Son, Ltd., of London, England, we have secured the exclusive publishing rights for this book, as well as all others in THE MOTORCYCLIST'S LIBRARY.

Included in THE MOTORCYCLIST'S LIBRARY are complete instruction manuals covering the care and operation of respective motorcycles and engines; valuable data on speed tuning, and thrilling accounts of motorcycle race events. See listing of available titles elsewhere in this edition.

We consider it a privilege to be able to offer so many fine titles to our customers.

FLOYD CLYMER
Publisher of Books Pertaining to Automobiles and Motorcycles
2125 W. PICO ST.   LOS ANGELES 6, CALIF.

INTRODUCTION

Welcome to the world of digital publishing ~ the book you now hold in your hand, while unchanged from the original edition, was printed using the latest state of the art digital technology. The advent of print-on-demand has forever changed the publishing process, never has information been so accessible and it is our hope that this book serves your informational needs for years to come. If this is your first exposure to digital publishing, we hope that you are pleased with the results. Many more titles of interest to the classic automobile and motorcycle enthusiast, collector and restorer are available via our website at **www.VelocePress.com**. We hope that you find this title as interesting as we do.

NOTE FROM THE PUBLISHER

The information presented is true and complete to the best of our knowledge. All recommendations are made without any guarantees on the part of the author or the publisher, who also disclaim all liability incurred with the use of this information.

TRADEMARKS

We recognize that some words, model names and designations, for example, mentioned herein are the property of the trademark holder. We use them for identification purposes only. This is not an official publication.

INFORMATION ON THE USE OF THIS PUBLICATION

This manual is an invaluable resource for the classic **BSA** enthusiast and a "must have" for owners interested in performing their own maintenance. However, in today's information age we are constantly subject to changes in common practice, new technology, availability of improved materials and increased awareness of chemical toxicity. As such, it is advised that the user consult with an experienced professional prior to undertaking any procedure described herein. While every care has been taken to ensure correctness of information, it is obviously not possible to guarantee complete freedom from errors or omissions or to accept liability arising from such errors or omissions. Therefore, any individual that uses the information contained within, or elects to perform or participate in do-it-yourself repairs or modifications acknowledges that there is a risk factor involved and that the publisher or its associates cannot be held responsible for personal injury or property damage resulting from the use of the information or the outcome of such procedures.

It is important that the reader recognizes that any instructions may refer to either the right-hand or left-hand sides of the vehicle or the components and that the directions are followed carefully. One final word of advice, this publication is intended to be used as a reference guide, and when in doubt the reader should consult with a qualified technician.

Preface

B.S.A. O.H.V. vertical twin motor-cycles need no introduction: their attractive appearance, silky running, economy, reliability, and sparkling performance are widely known and greatly appreciated.

The 497 c.c. Model A7 Twin was introduced first and proved an immediate success. The more powerful 646 c.c. Model A10 (Golden Flash) quickly followed and proved equally successful. From 1951–1962 the power units of *all* A7, A10 vertical twins have been of the same general design, many major components being actually interchangeable. During recent years various minor modifications have been embodied, and these have still further improved general performance and efficiency. Few improvements have been found necessary, but all recent A10 models have micro-Babbit big-end liners and a reinforced crankshaft. All A7 and A10 models also have full-width hubs of cast iron.

The general specification of all the B.S.A. O.H.V. vertical twins is very similar, but there are certain variations on different models. For instance, some engines are of the "sports" type having high-compression pistons, a light-alloy cylinder head, sports-type camshaft, etc. Most 1948–54 models have plunger-type rear springing, but all the later models embody "swinging arm" rear suspension.

In 1962 the two entirely new 499 c.c. and 654 c.c. Models A50 and A65 were introduced. These both have unit-construction engines and gear-boxes and their general design differs considerably from the A7 and A10 designs. Model A10 was discontinued in 1963, and Model A7 dropped in 1962. Considerations of space do not permit of the author dealing with Models A50 and A65. The objective of this maintenance handbook is to help you to obtain and maintain the maximum mileage, maximum efficiency, minimum fuel consumption, and lowest running costs from your B.S.A. Twin. *It contains essential maintenance instructions for all 1948–62 500 c.c., 650 c.c. A7 and A10 O.H.V. vertical twins*: where maintenance instructions are not specifically dated or named, they are applicable to *all* B.S.A. vertical twins.

In conclusion I thank B.S.A. Motor Cycles, Ltd. of Birmingham 11, for their generous assistance with regard to technical data and for permitting various B.S.A. illustrations to be reproduced. I also thank various accessory firms for their kind co-operation.

W. C. H.

Contents

1 Handling a B.S.A. Twin 1
2 The Amal Carburettor 19
3 Care of Lighting System 39
4 Correct Lubrication 59
5 General Maintenance 75
   Index 132

1 Handling a B.S.A. Twin

It is assumed that you have purchased brand new or second-hand one of the now very popular 500 c.c. or 650 c.c. O.H.V. vertical twin B.S.A. models, and wish to get on the road as soon as possible.

B.S.A. twins are all very easy to handle and inspire confidence immediately, even in the veriest novice. Whether experienced or not, it is advisable to buy and read thoroughly a copy of the 32-page booklet, *The Highway Code*, and also a copy of the smaller booklet, *The New Traffic Signs*. Both are profusely illustrated, published by H.M. Stationery Office, and obtainable from most booksellers at 6d. each.

Essential Preliminaries. You are *not* permitted by law to ride a solo motor-cycle or a sidecar outfit on the public highway until certain legal preliminaries have been complied with. You must—

1. Take out a good insurance policy covering all *third-party* risks, and obtain the vital "certificate of insurance." With a brand new machine obtain a "cover note" pending the allocation of a registration number and the subsequent issue of the insurance policy and the "certificate." If your B.S.A. vertical twin is worth a considerable sum (and it probably is) it is clearly advisable to take out a full comprehensive insurance policy. If you buy a mount brand new or secondhand on deferred terms, you will probably have no option in the matter.

2. Obtain the registration book and the registration licence (Form VE 1/2,* or renew the licence (Form VE 1/A). All B.S.A. vertical twins are taxed at the rate of £10 per annum (no extra if a sidecar is fitted).

3. Obtain a *provisional* (six months) or a *qualified* (three years) driving licence (Form D.L.I.). The driving licence† *must be signed* immediately it is issued. Note that you are not entitled to any driving licence until you are sixteen years of age and have also complied with one of the following two conditions—

(*a*) You have held a licence (other than a provisional or Visitor's

---

* On Form R.F. 1/2 (required for original registration or change of ownership) you must state the engine and frame identification markings (e.g., AA7–5001 and ZA76–26001) situated on the near side of the crankcase, and on the near side of the steering-head lug at the top of the front down-tube respectively.

† The costs of provisional and three-year qualified driving licences are 10s. and 15s. respectively.

licence), authorizing the driving of vehicles of the class or description applied for, within a period of ten years ending on the date of coming into force of the licence applied for.

(*b*) You have passed the prescribed driving test which costs £1 15s. (Form D.L. 26) during the said period of ten years.

4. If not already provided, fit a red reflector (of 1½ in. minimum diameter) vertically at the rear of the motor-cycle, and in the case of a sidecar

Fig. 1. A Most Exhilarating O.H.V. Twin Suitable for Fast Solo, Pillion, or Sidecar Work—the 650 c.c. Model A10 Super Rocket

This renowned 650 c.c. B.S.A. O.H.V. vertical twin has a specially tuned and brake-tested engine with high-compression pistons, light-alloy cylinder head, and sports-type camshaft. It has a superb performance on the open road and good traffic manners. The 650 c.c. Model A10 Golden Flash has a rather similar general specification, but has a cast-iron cylinder head and standard-type camshaft; the same applies to the 500 c.c. Model A7 O.H.V. Twin, but the 500 c.c. Model A7 Shooting Star has the Super Rocket sports-type characteristics.

outfit an additional red reflector at the rear of the sidecar and at the same height as the reflector on the motor-cycle.

5. Mount "L" plates at the front and rear, if you are eligible for a provisional licence only; then do not ride a machine over 250 c.c.

6. If you hold only a provisional licence and carry a pillion passenger, see that he or she holds a current driving licence.

Note that all the official forms previously mentioned are obtainable from a money-order post office. Although not legally obliged to wear a crash helmet, buy a good type and *always* wear it while riding. It is not expensive and can prevent serious head injury in the event of an accident. *See* also page 18.

The Riding Position. It is advisable to make quite sure right from the start that the riding position *is* comfortable, and that the various controls come readily to hand. On a new vertical twin the standard riding position is generally found to be correct for a man of average build but, to suit a rider who is not of average physique, a combined adjustment can be made in respect of: (*a*) the angle of the handlebars, (*b*) the angle of the control levers on the handlebars, (*c*) the footrest position, and (*d*) the position of the foot gear-change pedal. Where a saddle is provided (on many earlier models), this is adjustable for height, but no adjustment of a dualseat position is possible.

(*a*) To adjust the handlebars for angle, loosen the four clamp bolts and (while astride the saddle or dualseat) move the handlebars until the best angle is obtained. The arms should normally be *almost straight*. After adjusting the handlebar position as required, be sure to re-tighten the four clamp bolts very securely.

(*b*) To position the handlebar controls so that the levers come readily to hand, loosen the clip securing-screws and then move the control assemblies to the most convenient positions within the limits provided. Verify that the throttle twist-grip has sufficient friction. The friction adjuster is located on the under side of the twist-grip at its inner end. Also check that there is no slackness in the throttle and air controls. An adjuster is conveniently provided near the handlebar end of each control cable.

(*c*) To adjust the footrests (the angle between the thigh and the leg should be *slightly less than a right-angle*), use the following procedure on all models not equipped with "swinging arm" rear suspension. Slacken the nuts holding the footrest hangers to the tapered sleeves and move the footrest hangers to give the most comfortable position. Both footrests must, of course, be positioned at exactly the same height, and the two securing nuts must be tightened very firmly. Note that the off-side nut has a *left-hand thread*.

To adjust the footrests on models equipped with "swinging arm" rear suspension, slacken the nut on the long bolt holding both footrests. Then tap out the bolt far enough to enable the footrest arms to be knocked off the parallel serrated shafts pegged to the frame. The footrest arms can then be replaced in the most convenient position and the long bolt firmly re-tightened.

(*d*) To adjust the position of the foot gear-change pedal, slacken the lever pinch-bolt and then alter the position of the lever on its splined shaft, so that easy pivotal action of the foot about the off-side footrest effects all upward and downward gear changes. Normally the gear-change lever should be inclined slightly downwards, and it is generally inadvisable to alter its original position.

(*e*) To adjust the saddle height (where a saddle is fitted), loosen the nuts on the saddle-spring pillars, raise or lower the saddle as desired, and then re-tighten securely the spring securing-nuts. As previously mentioned, no adjustment is possible where a dualseat is fitted.

LAYOUT AND USE OF CONTROLS

Before attempting to start up, you should, if you have never before handled a B.S.A. O.H.V. vertical twin, get thoroughly familiar with the layout and use of the various controls, most of which are attached to the handlebars.

It is assumed that you are familiar with the general principles of the four-stroke petrol engine and understand the purpose of the engine controls which are basically similar on all motor-cycles, except for some slight variations. For instance, there is no exhaust-valve lifter fitted on B.S.A. twins. It is a good plan to sit on the saddle or dualseat and "twiddle" the various levers while meditating on what would happen with the engine in motion.

The neatly arranged controls (*see* Figs. 2 and 3) may conveniently be divided into three groups; (1) engine controls, (2) motor-cycle controls, and (3) electrical controls.

1. The Engine Controls. These are: (*a*) the throttle twist-grip, (*b*) the air lever, (*c*) the ignition lever (where fitted), and (*d*) the ignition cut-out button.

The throttle twist-grip (controlling engine power) has a full movement of about a quarter of a turn (about half a turn, 1955 onwards) and is opened by *inward* movement (towards you).

The air lever which controls the admission of air into the carburettor mixing-chamber should normally be kept *wide open*. When starting the engine from *cold*, however, the air lever should be *fully closed*.

An ignition lever (*see* Fig. 2) is provided on the near side of the handlebars on 1953–9 sports-type O.H.V. vertical twins (the Shooting Star, Road Rocket, Super Rocket, etc.), but the standard-type 500 c.c. Model A7 Twin and the 650 c.c. Model A10 Golden Flash have automatic ignition-advance mechanism embodied in the timing case. *Outward* movement of the ignition lever (away from you) *advances* the ignition timing, and inward movement retards it.* Except for starting-up purposes it is important always to keep the ignition lever (where fitted) advanced as far as possible.

The ignition cut-out button on the 1948–50 Model A7 Twin is located on the cover of the magneto contact-breaker. On later A7 and A10 models the button is positioned on the handlebars (*see* Figs. 2 and 3), either on the near side (1951–2 models) or at, or near, the centre (1953–9 models). An exhaust-valve lifter is not fitted or required; it is only necessary to press the cut-out button for a second to stop the engine when the throttle is set to give a reliable tick-over with the throttle twist-grip fully closed.

* On 1955–9 A7 and A10 models with manual ignition-control, the cable operating the cam return-spring on the magneto is freed from tension when the ignition lever is fully *advanced*. On 1953–4 models, however, the tension is released when the ignition lever is fully *retarded*.

2. The Motor-cycle Controls. These are: (*a*) the foot gear-change pedal, (*b*) the clutch lever, (*c*) the front-brake lever, (*d*) the rear-brake pedal, and (*e*) the steering damper.

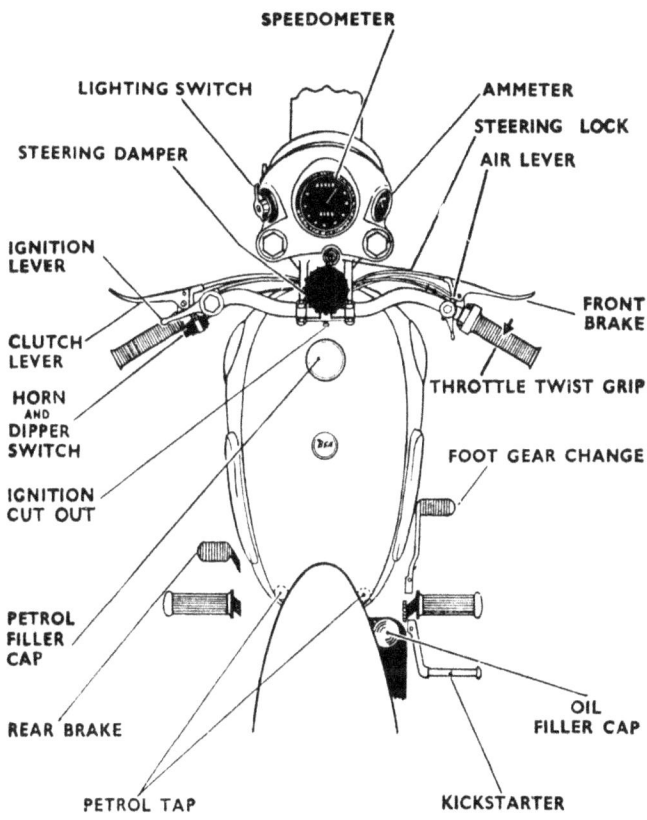

FIG. 2. LAYOUT OF HANDLEBAR CONTROLS (1953–9)

An ignition lever is fitted only on the Shooting Star, Road Rocket, and Super Rocket models. On 1958–9 machines the lighting switch and ammeter are on the off-side and near-side respectively. The 1959–62 cut-out is on the dipper switch and the 1961–2 air lever below the dualseat nose.

The B.S.A. foot gear-change mechanism is of the positive-stop type and gives nice, easy selection of the gears. The gear-change pedal (*see* Fig. 5) must always be raised or depressed *fully* when changing down or up respectively. Note that the pedal on the B.S.A. four-speed gearbox always returns to the *same position* after each gear is engaged, ready for the next engagement. Neutral is between first and second gear. Remember that excessive pressure must *never* be applied to the foot gear-change pedal, otherwise damage may be caused.

The clutch lever must always be fully squeezed to disengage the clutch (and thereby disconnect the engine power from the rear wheel) prior to

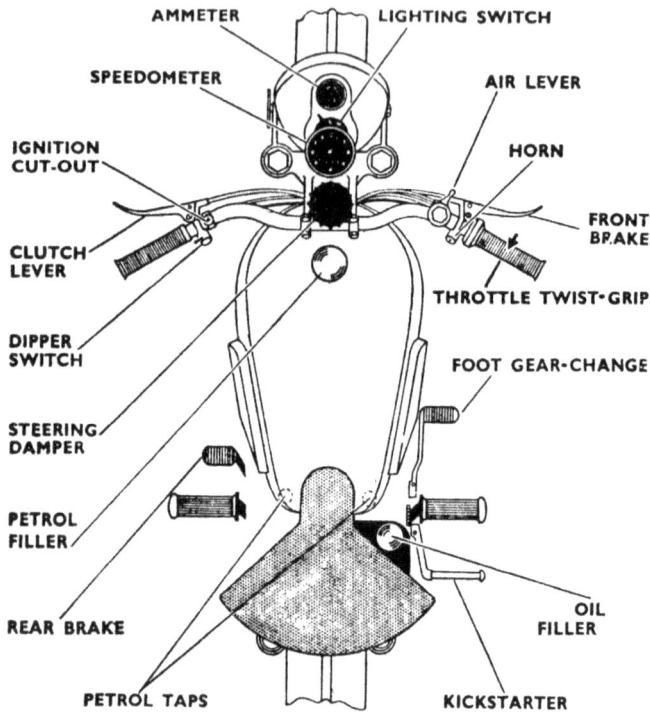

Fig. 3. Layout of Controls on 1948–52 500, 600 c.c. B.S.A. Twins (Models A7 and A10)

On the 1948–50 Model A7 twin, the ignition cut-out button is mounted on the magneto contact-breaker cover, very accessible to the rider's left hand.

raising or depressing the foot gear-change pedal. When the required gear is engaged, the clutch lever must be released slowly and *progressively* to re-engage the clutch plates and allow the engine power to be transmitted to the rear wheel via the secondary chain. Beware fierce application of the clutch, this being bad for both the engine and transmission.

Powerful large-diameter internal-expanding brakes are provided for both wheels. On most recent models full-width brake shoes are specified. Note that to bring the motor-cycle to a halt, it is the best policy to apply the front and rear brakes *simultaneously*.

The steering characteristics of all B.S.A. O.H.V. vertical twins are excellent and when riding a solo model it should normally be unnecessary to tighten down the steering damper except when travelling over very rough roads or when travelling very fast. When riding a solo model at very low speeds it is essential to keep the damper slackened right off, otherwise the steering may be adversely affected. With a sidecar outfit, on the other hand, the steering damper can always be kept slightly tightened down with no ill effects. The sports models, such as the Super Rocket, now have a metal stop contacting the edge of the damper. This eliminates any risk of the damper slackening off when travelling at very high speed on the open road.

3. **The Electrical Controls.** Disregarding ignition, these comprise; (*a*) the lighting switch, (*b*) the dipper switch, and (*c*) the horn button.

The lighting switch has three positions (*see* page 49) and is mounted on a panel at the rear of the headlamp behind the ammeter except on 1953-62 models where it is positioned on the near side (the off-side, 1958-62) of the headlamp cowl close to the speedometer.

The dipper switch on all models is on the near side of the handlebars at the rear of the clutch lever. It controls the double-filament main bulb in the Lucas headlamp and provides the normal driving light or the dipped beam as required.

The horn button on 1948-54 A7 and A10 models is fitted at the rear of the front-brake lever. On 1955-62 models the dipper switch and horn button are combined to form a single unit (*see* Fig. 2).

The Ammeter. This is mounted forward on a panel on top of the Lucas headlamp, except on 1953-62 models where it is mounted on the headlamp cowl on the opposite side to the lighting switch. It indicates at a glance whether the dynamo is charging the battery or whether the battery is being discharged. Note that with compensated-voltage-control the dynamo charge is variable (*see* page 42) irrespective of dynamo speed, but unless the battery is charged to maximum capacity, at least a trickle charge should always be indicated by the ammeter needle when the engine is running with all lamps switched off.

The Speedometer. A Smiths trip-type 120 m.p.h. speedometer is mounted above the front forks, or is recessed into the headlamp cowl on 1953-62 models (*see* Fig. 2). A white line indicates the 30 m.p.h. calibration, and the needle should not pass this mark in "built-up" areas having a 30 m.p.h. speed limit, and preferably not anywhere during the running-in period, though in this instance the actual throttle opening is the most important factor (*see* page 17).

On a model with the speedometer mounted on the headlamp cowl, in order to turn back the trip mileage recorder to zero, pull out the spring-loaded flexible control below the cowl and turn it *clockwise* as required.

The Spring-up Central Stand. All B.S.A. vertical twins have this type of stand in addition to a front stand. The knack of easily pulling the machine backwards and upwards with the lifting handle, while holding the leg of the central stand firm with the foot, is quickly mastered. All 1958–9 models have a new design of easy-action roll-on central stand and this requires little effort to operate.

To remove the machine from the central stand, it is only necessary to push the machine forward, when the stand automatically springs upwards well clear of the ground.

When Using a Prop Stand. A prop stand is fitted by many B.S.A. owners. When using it, always turn off the petrol to prevent the risk of the carburettor flooding, and for obvious reasons do not use a prop stand on soft ground (including a tarred road surface in hot weather). The result is often deplorable.

The Two Petrol Taps. Two flexible petrol pipes and two taps (*see* Fig. 4) are fitted. Both taps are located beneath the rear of the petrol tank and control the main fuel supply. If one tap is kept turned off, a reserve petrol supply is maintained in the tank, this reserve supply being fed to the carburettor float-chamber only when the second tap is turned on. For obvious reasons it is always desirable to maintain a reserve petrol supply while riding.

On 1948–52 B.S.A. twins with push-pull type taps, to close either petrol tap, push the *serrated* button in; to open the tap, push the *hexagon* button in.

On all 1953–62 B.S.A. twins, in order to close either petrol tap, turn its button *clockwise* and push in; to open the tap, pull its button out and lock by turning *anti-clockwise*.

REPLENISHMENT

Replenishing Petrol Tank. Always replenish the petrol tank with good premium-grade petrol. Never fill up with poor quality fuel. On the earlier 500 c.c. A7 models with plunger-type rear springing the capacity of the petrol tank is $3\frac{1}{2}$ gallons. On the earlier 650 c.c. A10 models with similar type rear springing the petrol tank capacity is $4\frac{1}{4}$ gallons. In the case of all later A7 and A10 models with "swinging arm" rear suspension the petrol tank holds no less than 4 gallons.

During the running-in period (about 1,500 miles), and also afterwards, it is very beneficial (except possibly where a specially tuned and brake-tested sports engine, such as the Super Rocket, is concerned) to add a shot of upper-cylinder lubricant, such as Redex, to each gallon of petrol poured into the tank. Some riders as an alternative add an egg-cupful of engine oil to each two gallons of petrol, but the former method is definitely preferable and simpler.

Replenishing Oil Tank. With regard to oil replenishment, suitable brands and grades of engine oils are recommended on page 60. The capacity of the oil tank on most earlier twins with plunger-type rear springing is about 4 pints. On all later twins with "swinging arm" type rear suspension the oil tank capacity is increased to $5\frac{1}{2}$ pints. Avoid replenishing with

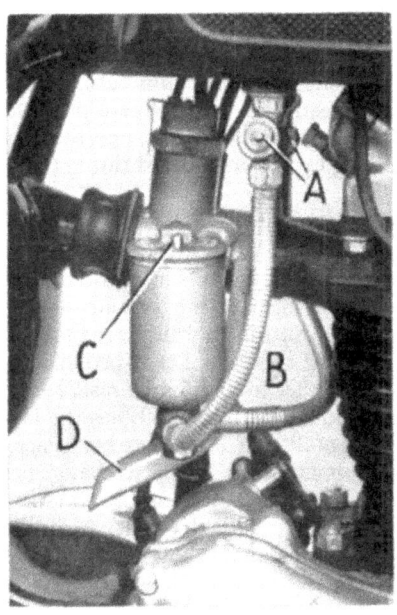

FIG. 4. SHOWING THE TWIN PETROL FEED, TAPS, ETC.
A top petrol-feed is provided on 1955–9 models with Amal "monobloc" carburettors. Note the useful drip shield.
    A. Petrol taps
    B. Twin petrol pipes joined at banjo union
    C. Float-chamber tickler (standard-type carburettor)
    D. Drip shield

winter grade engine oil during the summer months, as this grade is appreciably thinner than the summer grade and during summer the engine often runs a little hotter.

After the initial filling, inspect the oil level frequently and top-up the tank whenever necessary to within about *one inch* from the oil-return pipe orifice. The minimum safe oil level is indicated on the outside of the oil tank (*see* page 59). On a twin having a new or reconditioned engine, it is advisable to change the engine oil after covering 250 miles (*see* page 62).

Replenishing Gearbox, Oil-bath Chain Case, etc. Be sure that the gearbox always contains sufficient engine oil (*see* page 68), and check that the level of oil in the oil-bath chain case (*see* page 67) is adequate. Various other lubrication points require regular attention with the oil-can or the grease-gun as described in Chapter IV.

Replenishment on a New A7 or A10. When a new or good secondhand machine is obtained or ridden away from a reputable dealer, it is, of course, the normal practice for the dealer to attend to the proper replenishment of the oil tank, gearbox, and oil-bath chain case, and also to see that the battery is filled and correctly charged. Where practicable, the dealer also deals with many of the legal preliminaries, and the new owner has little to attend to before starting up the engine and riding the machine for the first time.

STARTING UP ENGINE

Setting Controls for Starting Up. Any motor-cyclist, whether experienced or not, will soon master the correct setting of the controls on a B.S.A. vertical twin, necessary to ensure an easy and quick start in all weather conditions. The correct control procedure is as follows—

1. Fully open *one* of the two petrol taps provided (*see* page 8), leaving the second tap closed in order to maintain a reserve supply of petrol in the petrol tank. The best policy is always to open the tap on the *left*, as this greatly reduces the possibility of both taps being accidentally opened.

2. Make absolutely sure that the foot gear-change pedal has been moved to obtain neutral (between first and second gears). A neutral indicator is *not* provided; therefore in a practical manner verify that the rear wheel is disconnected from the engine and able to rotate freely. If the machine is on its central stand, spin the wheel by hand; otherwise move the machine forward and note if there is any resistance caused by the engine.

3. Open (*anti-clockwise*) the throttle twist-grip very slightly. Measured at the rim of the twist-grip rubber, the movement should not exceed $\frac{1}{8}$ in.

4. If the engine is *quite cold*, close the air lever *completely*. Should the engine still be *thoroughly warm*, open the air lever fully. Where the engine is *only slightly warm* (after being stopped for a limited period), it is usually necessary to close the air lever slightly, the amount of closing desirable best being determined by practical experience and depending to some extent on the actual engine temperature.

5. Retard the ignition lever (where fitted) slightly to avoid the possibility of a kick-back.

Starting Up. With the various controls correctly set for starting as previously described, slightly flood the carburettor *if the engine is quite cold* by depressing *momentarily* the tickler (*see* Fig. 4) on top of the carburettor float-chamber. Never depress the tickler for longer than about a second, as excessive flooding invariably causes difficult starting.

Push down the kick-starter until resistance is felt and while sitting astride the saddle or dualseat, deliver with the right foot a deliberate and vigorous downward thrust on the kick-starter pedal.

Your mount should normally fire at the first or second attempt, if it is new, or second-hand in good mechanical condition. As soon as the engine starts up, open the air lever progressively until it is *wide open*. Also advance the ignition lever (where fitted) until it is fully or almost fully advanced. Note that it is very bad to allow an engine to tick-over with the ignition appreciably retarded. Also remember that while riding, the air and ignition levers should with one exception *always* be kept fully open and advanced respectively.

When hill climbing at low speed with a higher gear engaged it is sometimes advisable to retard the ignition lever (where fitted) slightly, so as to ward off any detrimental tendency for knocking. On B.S.A. sports-type twins, such as the Super Rocket, in similar circumstances a slight gain in power may be obtained by also closing the air lever slightly.

Allow the engine to warm up at a moderate speed for a few minutes. Never permit the engine to race or tick-over too slowly with the engine-oil cold and not circulating effectively.

Note that warming up the engine too slowly is liable to cause incomplete combustion of atomized fuel above the pistons, with the result that some of the mixture condenses on, and corrodes, the cylinder walls. Technically, this is known as "low temperature condensation." Cease warming up the engine immediately it reaches its normal running temperature. Before riding a machine any appreciable distance, make a habit of removing the filler cap from the oil tank and observing whether oil is issuing steadily from the return-pipe orifice.

Refusal to Start Up. If your B.S.A. vertical twin fails to start up after making about four attempts with the kick-starter, it is probably that some minor defect is responsible. Check the following points—

1. Verify that the engine control setting *is* correct. Note that to induce a high-velocity air stream over the pilot jet, it is *essential* to open the throttle a *very slight amount*.

2. Check that when the carburettor float-chamber tickler is held depressed for some seconds, petrol begins to drip down the drip-shield (D, Fig. 4) from the base of the carburettor. Also ascertain whether flooding occurs when the finger is removed from the tickler. It should stop quickly, provided that there is no float-chamber defect.

3. If the fuel system appears to be quite in order, remove both sparking plugs, clean them, check their gaps, and test the plugs for sparking before fitting them. If the plugs removed are found to be in poor condition and not capable of being rendered serviceable, fit two new plugs of the recommended make and type (*see* page 80).

Carburettor on Fire. A sticking inlet valve or a back-fire on rare occasions starts a carburettor blaze. In this very remote event, both petrol taps should be shut and the engine run fast to exhaust the petrol remaining in the float-chamber and fuel pipes. The alternative is to use a fire-extinguisher.

ON THE ROAD

With the engine ticking-over moderately fast and neutral engaged, ease the machine gently off its central stand, assuming this was used for starting up.

To Engage First Gear. Now sitting astride the machine in a relaxed position, disengage the clutch by squeezing the clutch lever on the near side of the handlebars. Then with the toe of the foot *raise* the foot gear-change pedal *fully* and engage first (bottom) gear. To facilitate proper engagement with the machine stationary, it may be necessary to move the motor-cycle backwards and forwards slightly while maintaining a light pressure with the foot on the gear-change pedal. When properly selected, you should *feel* first gear engage. This also applies to the remaining gears.

Sticking Plates on a New B.S.A. Twin. On a brand new machine slight sticking of the clutch plates occasionally causes some initial difficulty in engaging first gear, but this trouble quickly disappears with use. If such initial difficulty does occur, stop the engine by pressing the ignition cut-out button (*see* page 4) and smartly operate the kick-starter pedal several times with the clutch fully disengaged, so as to free the clutch plates.

Moving Off. After engaging first (bottom) gear, open the throttle slightly and allow the transmission to transmit engine power to the rear wheel by gently and progressively releasing the clutch lever. Do not allow the clutch to slip for longer than is necessary while gear changing or at any other time. As soon as the clutch is engaged you should move off quite smoothly.

As your motor-cycle moves forward and engine power takes the full load, gradually open the throttle more, so as to accelerate the machine until a suitable road speed is attained for changing up into second gear (*see* Fig. 5).

On those 1953-9 sports-type vertical twins having manual control of the ignition, move the ignition lever (away from you) as far as possible to the *full advance* position if it is not already in this position, which it should be. Also verify that the air lever is wide open where it should remain while riding (*see* note on page 11).

Changing Up. When you have attained a moderate speed, change up into second gear. With the B.S.A. constant-mesh four-speed gearbox, gear crashing is impossible, and the technique of good gear changing is soon mastered.

Throttle down the engine slightly and simultaneously disengage the clutch by squeezing the clutch lever. Pause a split-second and depress the foot gear-change pedal to its *full extent* with toe pressure until second gear is *felt* to engage. Then re-engage the clutch quickly and progressively, remove the toe from the foot gear-change pedal, and permit the pedal to return to its normal position, ready for the next upward change. To compensate for the increased load taken by the engine, open the throttle slightly immediately after changing up into second gear.

To change up into third and fourth (top) gears, use the same procedure as that just described for changing up into second, but make the changes

FIG. 5. THE B.S.A. FOUR-SPEED GEARBOX AND FOOT GEAR-CHANGE

When changing up or down, the gear-change pedal is depressed or raised to its full extent as indicated by the arrows.

at appropriately higher speeds. Always change gear at a sufficient road speed, but avoid revving the engine unnecessarily fast when accelerating between the gear changes. On no account apply excessive pressure to the foot gear-change pedal, and when changing up or down always maintain a light pressure on the gear-change pedal until the clutch has been firmly re-engaged.

Changing Down. To change down from fourth (top) gear into third gear, partly close the throttle until your B.S.A. twin is moving at a speed which is normal cruising speed for third gear. Simultaneously disengage the clutch and open the throttle slightly. Pause a split-second and then *raise* the foot gear-change pedal to its *full extent* with toe pressure until third gear is *felt* to engage. Immediately afterwards close the throttle to its normal position, re-engage the clutch, and remove the toe from the gear-change pedal. As soon as third gear is engaged, open the throttle slightly to compensate for the increase in engine speed relative to that of the rear wheel.

To change down into second and first gears, proceed in a manner similar to that used for changing down into third gear, raising the gear-change pedal fully during each change. Note that, except when hill climbing, it is not necessary when changing down from fourth or third gear into first gear to complete the full gear-changing procedure for each intermediate gear change. You can throttle down until the machine is travelling very slowly, and then disengage the clutch and raise the gear-change pedal fully twice or three times in quick succession, according to whether third or fourth gear was previously engaged. "Blip" (i.e. throttle up) the engine slightly during each movement of the gear-change pedal. Having engaged the desired gear, close the throttle to its normal position, re-engage the clutch, and finally open the throttle until the appropriate road speed is obtained.

To Obtain "Neutral." Change down into first (bottom) gear, brake the machine to a stop with the engine ticking over and the throttle twist-grip closed, disengage the clutch, and then *depress* the foot gear-change pedal gently and *very slightly* until the pedal is felt to click into the correct position. "Neutral" is located between first and second gears. If by accident you depress the foot gear-change pedal fully, you will, of course, engage second gear.

For the novice to verify that he is actually in "neutral," it is advisable to let in the clutch very gradually. When you become a really accomplished rider (and not before) you can, if you wish, learn to engage "neutral" with the machine still on the move. Doing this, however, requires considerable precision of control and confidence.

Correct Use of Brakes. To get the maximum retardation with the minimum wear of the brake linings and tyres, it is advisable to acquire the habit of always applying the front and rear brakes simultaneously. Do not, however, brake unnecessarily or excessively, as this necessarily submits the tyres and transmission to unfair wear and tear.

When descending steep gradients it is good policy to make full use of engine compression as a brake by closing the throttle and opening the air lever wide. In no circumstances use the clutch or the ignition cut-out button for controlling speed. Wherever possible, control speed solely by making good use of the throttle, using the brakes as little and seldom as possible.

To Stop Your Motor-cycle. A novice should note that the normal procedure for stopping on the road is as follows—

1. Close the throttle completely.
2. Fully disengage the clutch.
3. Apply the front and rear brakes simultaneously, and progressively increase the hand and foot pressure as required.

4. As the machine stops, change down into first gear and engage "neutral."

5. Press the ignition cut-out button for a second, if you desire to stop the engine.

Practise gear changing and stopping the motor-cycle until what at first seems a complicated procedure can be effected with precision and very quickly. It is definitely unsafe to venture on to congested roads until your sub-conscious mind can take control of all essential quick movements. If an emergency arises there is no time to think consciously about what to do and how to do it. You just have to do it automatically and extremely quickly!

Advice on Hill Climbing. It is important when ascending hills always to maintain the engine revolutions (r.p.m.) reasonably high by making full use of the four-speed gearbox, especially if a sidecar is attached to your mount. Do not permit the engine to labour or knock, and therefore always change down to a lower gear *in good time*. Use a good throttle opening and on 1953-9 sports-type twins (e.g., the Super Rocket), retard the ignition only when this becomes necessary (*see* page 11).

Close the throttle fully and open the air lever wide when descending steep hills, thereby making full use of engine compression as a brake and effectively cooling the engine at the same time. Note that it is pleasant, but technically illegal, to coast downhill in "neutral." Never attempt this on a really steep hill, and always brake the motor-cycle to a stop before engaging first gear.

Parking Your Machine. Down-draught Amal standard-type or "monobloc" carburettors are fitted to *all* B.S.A. vertical twins, and therefore there is a natural tendency for neat petrol to enter the cylinders in the event of carburettor flooding occurring when the machine is left standing with the petrol turned on. This applies particularly to all the Road Rocket, Shooting Star, and Super Rocket models where the angle of carburettor inclination is somewhat steep. Always turn off the appropriate petrol tap (*see* page 8) when parking the machine, even for short periods.

When parking a B.S.A. twin by the roadside at night, always jack up the motor-cycle on its central or prop stand so that the *near side* of the machine is adjacent to the kerb, and keep the pilot light switched on unless the motor-cycle is well illuminated by a street lamp. Where a machine is left unattended for long periods it is advisable to take reasonable precautions against the risk of theft.

A suitable padlock and chain can be used for locking the front wheel, but all 1955 and later twins have an ingenious built-in locking device operated by a Yale key (*see* Fig. 6) and it is a simple matter to lock the steering at an acute angle, rendering it quite impossible for anyone to ride or wheel the motor-cycle away, provided that the Yale key is removed.

To operate the built-in locking device, turn the handlebars so that the front forks are moved over to the *left* and then turn the Yale key in the lock to release the plunger.

It is important not to insert oil into the keyhole of the built-in steering

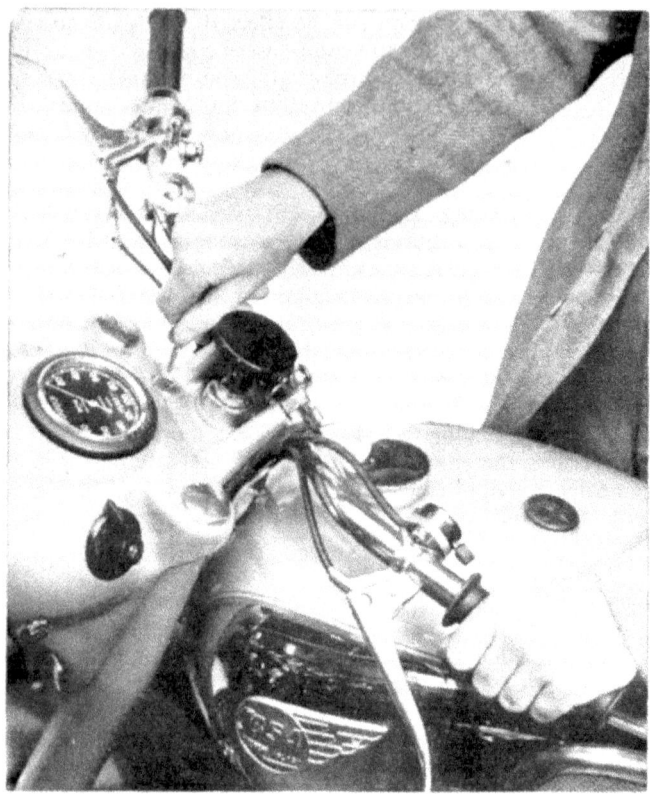

FIG. 6. LOCKING THE STEERING OF A B.S.A. TWIN TO PREVENT THEFT

After locking the steering be very careful not to lose the Yale key, otherwise you may be unable to move the machine.

lock, because this is liable to clog up the internal wards and wash away the special lubricant which is inserted before assembly. It is permissible, however, after completing a considerable mileage to apply a few drops of *thin machine oil* to the periphery of the moving drum. As regards the Yale key, it is obviously the safest plan to keep this attached to a key-ring. Its loss on the road can cause immense bother.

The Importance of Careful Running-in. This cannot be over emphasized. If you wish after running-in to obtain the maximum engine compression and high engine performance, always run-in a new or reconditioned engine with the *utmost care* during the first 1,000–1,500 miles running; and attend carefully to the correct lubrication of the engine and machine, and to general maintenance, dealt with in Chapters 4 and 5 respectively.

Go very easy on throttle openings during the running-in period, otherwise a new or reconditioned engine may be *permanently* spoiled. Until a mirror-like gloss and hardness spread over all bearing surfaces, and the vital oil film between moving parts reaches its peak of efficiency, careless running is liable to incur excessive friction and heat. Both are highly detrimental and can cause damage or even a seizure. Should an indication of impending piston seizure occur for any reason, *instantly* close the throttle and whip out the clutch. By doing this, serious damage can often be prevented and there may only be slight smearing on the lands between the piston rings, capable of being rectified by a skilled mechanic.

Until the running-in period is ended, do not use more than about *one-third* throttle in any gear, and make full use of the gearbox. Endeavour to make the engine run "light" as often as possible and avoid everything likely to cause excessive heat. Also avoid any rapid acceleration, and on no account permit the engine to labour while hill climbing; change down to a lower gear *in sufficient time*. As the running-in period nears completion, you may to advantage gradually increase the throttle openings, but do not turn the twist-grip to its full extent (avoid more than 45 m.p.h.) until your speedometer trip records 1,500 miles. Excessive full throttle is best avoided until you have covered 2,000 miles, and in the author's opinion it is best avoided at all times. Many unexpected things happen on the road and a moderate throttle opening enables them to be countered rather than encountered.

As has already been mentioned on page 8, it is sound policy when replenishing the petrol tank to add some upper-cylinder lubricant. Most garages have a device for squirting it into the tank, on request.

Always keep the oil tank and gearbox well topped-up (*see* pages 59 and 68). After covering 250 miles drain the oil tank, clean both filters, and replenish the tank with new oil of the appropriate type (*see* page 60). Repeat this procedure after riding 1,000 miles (thereafter repeat every 2,000 miles). Also drain and refill the gearbox after covering 500 miles (subsequently every 2,000 miles). For instructions, *see* page 70.

Remove and clean the sparking plug (*see* page 80) after covering about 1,000 miles. Some bedding-down of various parts occurs during the initial running-in, and it is advisable to check rather more frequently than usual the contact-breaker gap, the valve clearances, clutch adjustment, etc. At the same time check over the various external nuts and bolts for tightness (*see* Chapter 5).

Some Useful Riding Hints. Having had very considerable experience riding various types of motor-cycles on the road, the author offers the following general hints to B.S.A. twin owners, especially to youngsters learning to ride and those who have just passed their driving tests—

1. Before setting off on a long run, always satisfy yourself that your A7 or A10 *is* thoroughly road-worthy.

2. Always ride with due consideration for *all* road users, and conform with the law in both letter *and* spirit.

3. Avoid riding nose to tail. This is a dangerous practice.

4. Always assume that there *are* bad drivers on your route, and anticipate the unexpected.

5. Cultivate imagination. Note closely, and where possible foresee, the action of other road users.

6. Be particularly careful when negotiating cross-roads, especially in suburban areas, where priority roads are often not clearly marked, or not marked at all.

7. At all times, and especially at night and near hospitals. avoid making excessive and unnecessary noise. This habit gives us a bad name.

8. In "built-up" areas always keep your speed well within the margin of safety. 30 m.p.h. in the wrong place can be more dangerous than 70 m.p.h. in the right place!

9. Do not indulge in excessive "stunt" riding. This can bring disaster, though not necessarily for a long time!

10. Keep at a distance from lady "L" drivers in cars. Some are not mechanically minded, are slow to acquire road sense, and are apt to panic in an emergency. Others are quite good, but it is difficult to identify the two categories. Play for safety by keeping at a safe distance!

11. Always wear a crash helmet. Accidents to motor-cyclists often cause a bang on the head! Use and *keep* your brains!

Ministry of Transport Test Certificate. A Mot certificate for road worthiness must be obtained from an authorized garage, dealer, or repair shop in respect of any motor-cycle used in the U.K. which was first registered more than *three* years ago. Subsequently this certificate must be renewed *annually*. It must be produced when applying for a registration licence in respect of renewal or change of ownership (Forms VE 1/A and VE 1/2 respectively), together with a valid *certificate of insurance* and the current registration book.

The Mot certificate costs 10s. and it is legal to ride an *untaxed* motor-cycle to a suitable testing station after making an appointment for a test. The required certificate is issued on the spot if the motor-cycle passes the statutory test for the efficiency of the tyres, brakes, steering, lamps, horn, etc.

2 The Amal Carburettor

CORRECT carburation is vitally important to ensure good all-round engine performance. B.S.A. Motor Cycles, Ltd., have obtained and specified the very best carburettor settings after making exhaustive experiments and tests. It is therefore most unwise, and decidedly not beneficial, to attempt to alter the maker's settings. You should confine your attention to obtaining the best slow-running adjustment and to occasionally stripping-down the carburettor for thorough cleaning and careful inspection of its various components.

An Amal two-lever needle-jet carburettor is fitted to *all* Model A7 and A10 B.S.A. O.H.V. vertical twins. A standard-type instrument has been specified on all 1948–54 models distributed in the United Kingdom. On the 1949–50 Model A7 Star Twin, however, two standard-type Amal carburettors were fitted. The 1955 Model A10 Golden Flash with plunger-type rear springing also has a standard-type Amal carburettor. All other 1955–62 twins, provided with "swinging arm" rear suspension, have an Amal "monobloc" type carburettor fitted. This chapter deals with the standard type and the "monobloc" type carburettors.

STANDARD-TYPE CARBURETTOR

It is desirable that every motor-cyclist should understand the basic principles of the carburettor. An outline of the way in which the Amal carburettor functions is therefore included.

How It Works. On the standard-type needle-jet Amal carburettor the mixture at slow speeds and when ticking-over is regulated by a pilot jet which has an adjuster screw for controlling the admission of air and suction over the jet. At higher speeds the mixture strength is mainly controlled by a throttle valve and a tapered jet needle, attached to the throttle valve, working in a needle-jet. The main jet is located at the base of the needle-jet.

The standard-type Amal carburettor is for all practical purposes automatic, the air lever being closed only to facilitate starting from cold; but in certain circumstances (*see* page 11) it may be necessary to close it slightly while riding. The only external adjusters on the carburettor comprise the throttle-stop screw and the pilot-air adjusting screw. An adjustment of the former makes it possible for the engine to tick-over when the throttle twist-grip is *fully* closed, and an adjustment of the latter regulates the mixture strength for tick-over, and also for initial throttle openings up to about one-eighth throttle.

Referring to Fig. 7 showing a sectioned view of the standard-type carburettor, A is the carburettor body or mixing chamber, the upper part of which has a throttle slide or valve B with tapered jet needle C attached to the throttle valve by a needle clip. The throttle valve regulates the quantity of mixture supplied to the engine, and the jet needle C moves up and down with the throttle valve. Because the needle is tapered downwards, it allows more or less petrol to pass through the needle-jet O when the throttle is opened or closed respectively. Except at nearly full throttle and when idling, this applies throughout the range of throttle openings.

Passing through the throttle valve is the air valve D, independently operated and serving the purpose of obstructing the main air-passage for starting and mixture regulation. Fitted to the underside of the mixing chamber by the union nut E is the jet block F, and interposed between them is a fibre washer to ensure a petrol-tight joint.

On the upper part of the jet block is the adapter body H, forming a clean through-way. Integral with the jet block is the pilot jet J, supplied through the passage K. The adjustable pilot air-intake L communicates with a chamber, from which branches the pilot outlet M and the by-pass N. A throttle-stop screw (*see* Fig. 9, left-hand illustration) is provided on the side of the mixing chamber and, as already mentioned, controls the position of the throttle valve for tick-over. Convenient adjusters are provided for the throttle and air lever, close to the handlebar end of each control cable.

The needle-jet O is screwed into the base of the jet block, and carries at its bottom end the main jet P. Both jets can be removed when the jet plug Q (which firmly secures the float chamber to union nut E) is removed. The float chamber has a bottom petrol-feed and comprises a chamber R supplied with petrol through union S. The chamber contains the float T and the needle valve U attached to the float by the clip V. The float-chamber cover W has a lock-screw X to prevent loosening by vibration. Lock-ring Z (held by locking spring $Z1$) holds the mixing-chamber cap Y.

When the petrol tap is turned on, petrol flows past the needle valve U until the quantity of petrol in the float chamber R is high enough to raise the float T and allow the needle valve U to prevent further petrol entering the chamber until some has been sucked into the combustion chambers of the engine.

Petrol having filled the float chamber to the correct level, passes along the passages through the diagonal holes in the jet plug Q. These holes are in communication with the main jet P and the pilot feed-hole K. The petrol level in the needle-jet and pilot jet is therefore the same as the pre-determined level automatically maintained in the float chamber.

As regards the actual functioning of the carburettor, imagine the throttle valve B to be opened slightly. During each (downward) induction stroke of the pistons a partial vacuum is created in the carburettor, and this causes

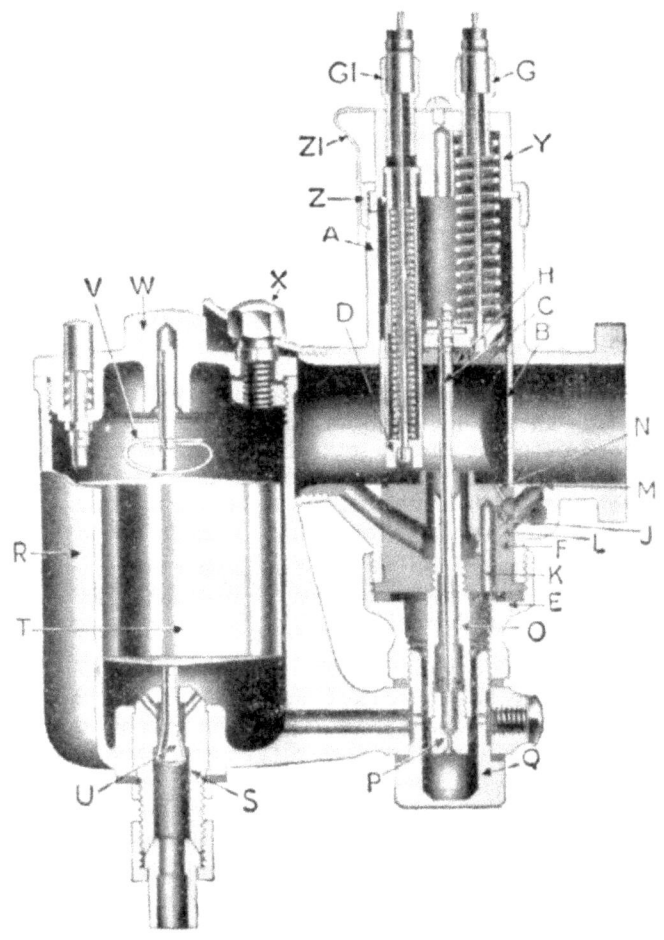

FIG. 7. SECTIONAL VIEW OF AMAL STANDARD-TYPE NEEDLE-JET CARBURETTOR

Fitted to 1948-54 twins and the 1955 Model A10 Golden Flash with plunger-type rear springing. The cable adjusters G. G1 are replaced by adjusters positioned near the handlebar control-cable ends.

Key to Fig. 7.

- A. Mixing chamber
- B. Throttle valve
- C. Jet needle and clip
- D. Air valve
- E. Union nut on A
- F. Jet block
- G. Cable adjuster (throttle
- G1. Cable adjuster (air)
- H. Adapter body
- J. Pilot jet
- K. Passage to J
- L. Pilot air-intake
- M. Pilot outlet
- N. Pilot by-pass
- O. Needle-jet
- P. Main jet
- Q. Jet plug
- R. Float chamber
- S. Float-chamber union
- T. Float
- U. Float needle valve
- V. Float-needle clip
- W. Float-chamber cover
- X. Lock-screw for W
- Y. Mixing-chamber cap
- Z. Lock ring for Y
- Z1. Locking spring for Y

a rush of air through the pilot air-intake L, and suction of petrol from the pilot jet J. The atomized mixture of air and petrol is admitted to the engine combustion chambers through the pilot outlet M.

The pilot outlet M is very small and is incapable of passing sufficient petrol to run the engine. The mixture is also excessively rich. Therefore it is necessary to raise throttle valve B slightly to admit a further supply of air from the main air-intake and obtain a properly proportioned mixture (about 13 parts of air to 1 of petrol) sufficient in quantity to run the engine. The greater is the opening of the throttle valve, the less is the depression caused on the outlet M, but, in turn, the bigger is the depression created on the by-pass N, and the pilot mixture flows from this passage as well as from the outlet M.

At about one-eighth throttle the mixture supplied by the pilot and by-pass system is supplemented by fuel from the main jet P. The throttle valve cut-away determines the mixture strength from one-eighth to one-quarter throttle. Continuing up the throttle range, mixture control by the jet-needle position occurs from one-quarter to three-quarters throttle. From this point the main jet alone is responsible for mixture regulation.

The air valve D is cable-operated from the handlebars and has the effect of obstructing the main through-way, thereby increasing the depression on the main jet, and so enriching the mixture.

The Main Jet. Referring to Fig. 7, the main jet is screwed into the needle-jet O and can readily be removed after unscrewing the jet plug. Referring to Fig. 9, to remove the main jet for cleaning and examination, hold the needle-jet with one spanner, and then with another spanner unscrew the main jet.

All Amal jets are calibrated and numbered to indicate their precise discharge. Thus any two jets with the same number marked on them are in all respects identical. Note that the larger the jet number, the larger is the jet orifice. When renewing a main jet, always fit one of the recommended size (*see* Tables I and II).

The Jet Needle. The position of the tapered jet needle attached to the throttle valve can after a big mileage sometimes be altered to reduce a high petrol consumption, but this procedure is not normally recommended. A thorough overhaul of the engine is likely to obtain the best results. The jet needle has five grooves for the clip. Needle position 3, the usual position recommended, means the *third groove from the top*. Lowering the jet needle in the throttle valve (and thus in the needle-jet) weakens the mixture, while raising the needle enriches the mixture.

"MONOBLOC"-TYPE CARBURETTOR

The "monobloc"-type Amal carburettor fitted to all 1955–62 B.S.A. O.H.V. vertical twins having "swinging arm" rear suspension, differs from the standard-type Amal carburettor in several respects, but its general method of functioning and adjustment is similar.

How It Works. The "monobloc" design includes; a horizontal float-chamber made integral with the main body of the carburettor, a small float-needle of moulded nylon, a top petrol feed with a gauze at the union, a needle-jet with bleed holes giving two-way compensation, and a pilot jet which can be readily removed for cleaning.

Details of the modified carburettor are shown in Fig. 8 which illustrates an exploded view of the instrument. Referring to Fig. 8, the float-chamber float 12 and the needle 8 maintain a constant level of petrol in the needle-jet 13 and the pilot jet 16, and cut off the petrol supply when the engine stops. Careful selection by the makers of the appropriate jet sizes and main choke bore ensures proper atomizing and proportioning of the petrol and air mixture sucked into the cylinders.

The air valve 2 is normally kept fully raised, and the throttle valve 23, controlled by the handlebar twist-grip, regulates the volume of mixture, and therefore the power output. At *all* throttle openings a correct mixture is automatically obtained.

The "monobloc" carburettor, like the standard instrument, operates in four stages. When opening the throttle from the fully closed position to one-eighth open (for tick-over) the mixture is supplied by the pilot jet 16, and the strength of the mixture is largely determined by the setting of the knurled pilot-air adjusting screw shown at 19 (*see also* Fig. 9). To facilitate adjustment of this screw, a coil spring is used instead of a lock-nut as hitherto, and the same applies to the throttle-stop adjusting screw 17. As the throttle is further slightly opened, the main-jet system comes into action, the mixture being augmented by the main jet 15 via the pilot by-pass.

The amount of cut-away on the atmospheric side of the throttle valve regulates the petrol to air ratio between one-eighth and one-quarter throttle. The needle-jet 13 and the jet needle 22 take over the mixture regulation between one-quarter and three-quarter throttle, and the mixture strength is determined by the relative position of the jet needle in the jet-needle clip 3 attached to the throttle valve 23.

When the throttle is opened beyond three-quarters, the mixture strength is determined only by the size of the main jet 15. Note that the main jet does not discharge petrol direct into the carburettor mixing-chamber, but discharges through the needle-jet 13 into the primary air-chamber. From there it enters the main choke through the primary air-choke. The latter has a compensating action in conjunction with the "bleed" holes in the needle-jet 13; this serves the dual purpose of air compensating the mixture from the needle-jet and allowing the fuel to form a well outside and around the needle-jet. This action improves acceleration at normal cruising speeds, and does not interfere with the functioning of the pilot jet and the main jet.

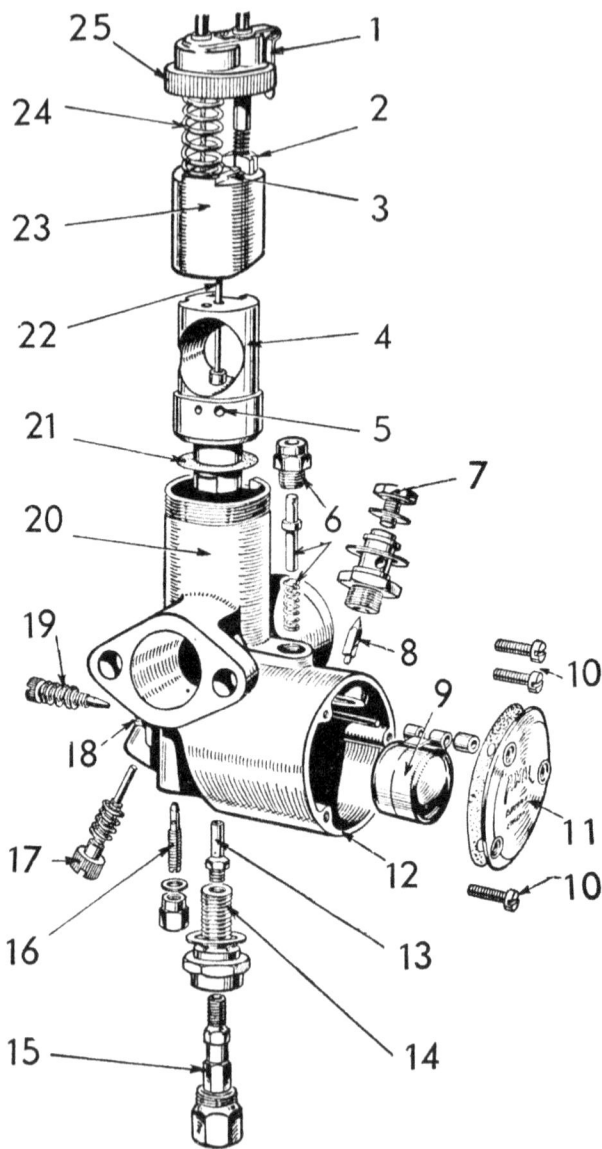

Fig. 8. Exploded View of Amal "Monobloc" type Needle-jet Carburettor (1955–62 Models)
(*By courtesy of B.S.A. Motor Cycles, Ltd.*)

THE AMAL CARBURETTOR

CARBURETTOR ADJUSTMENT (STANDARD AND "MONOBLOC" TYPES)

The maker's official carburettor settings (main-jet size, pilot-jet size, throttle valve, and needle position) are given in Tables I to III, and these correct settings should always be retained. No carburettor adjustment is normally necessary on a brand new model, but on a new machine which has done a considerable mileage, or on a second-hand machine, it is often advisable to adjust the pilot-jet and throttle-stop adjusting screws in order to obtain the very best petrol consumption and smooth slow-running and tick-over.

Note that an excessively rich slow-running mixture results in a tendency for the engine to run on the pilot jet under normal riding conditions. A weak slow-running mixture causes the engine to run hot and irregularly in the lower speed range. It is clear therefore that it is most important to obtain, and maintain, a correct slow-running mixture.

Evidence of a Correct Slow-running Mixture. If the carburettor setting and slow-running adjustment are correct, and the general condition of the carburettor is good, no black smoke should issue from the exhaust pipe when the throttle is sharply opened. With a *correct mixture*, the exhaust flame (observed at an open exhaust port) should be of a *whitish-blue* colour. The body of the sparking plug, when the latter is removed from a cylinder, should be black and bright. General performance in the lower speed range should be good and there should be no "flat spots" or "wooliness." Listen to the sound of the exhaust; it should be crisp and clear. With the mixture correct there should be no tendency for the engine to "spit-back" when ticking-over or while riding slowly.

With the mixture *too weak*, there is generally a pronounced tendency for the engine to "spit-back" and to overheat under slight provocation. General performance is also below standard. The exhaust flame at an open port is *light blue*. Should the mixture be excessively rich, petrol consumption is, of course, excessive and general performance is somewhat erratic. Generally some black smoke emerges from the exhaust when the throttle is opened sharply. Slight closing of the air lever will choke the

---

Key to Fig. 8.

1. Retaining spring for 25
2. Air valve
3. Jet-needle clip
4. Jet block
5. Pilot by-pass
6. Tickler assembly
7. Banjo securing-bolt
8. Float needle
9. Float
10. Float-chamber cover screws
11. Float-chamber cover
12. Float chamber
13. Needle jet

14. Main-jet holder
15. Main jet
16. Pilot jet
17. Throttle-stop adjusting screw
18. Locating screw for 4
19. Pilot-air adjusting screw
20. Body of carburettor
21. Fibre washer for 4
22. Jet needle
23. Throttle valve
24. Return spring for 23
25. Mixing-chamber cap ring

engine. With an excessively *rich mixture* the characteristic colour of the exhaust flame, at an open exhaust port, is *yellow*.

TABLE I. CARBURETTOR SETTINGS FOR 1955–9 MODELS
(SEE ALSO PAGE 38)

B.S.A. Model	Main Jet	Pilot Jet	Throttle Valve	Needle Position
A7 Twin	210	25	$3\frac{1}{2}$	2
A7 Shooting Star . .	270	30	$3\frac{1}{2}$	3
A10 Golden Flash . .	240	25	4	3*
A10 Road Rocket . .	340	—	6	4
A10 Super Rocket . .	240	25	$3\frac{1}{2}$	3
A10 Super Rocket 1959 .	400	30	$3\frac{1}{2}$	3

* On the 1958–9 A10 Golden Flash the needle position is No. 2.

TABLE II. CARBURETTOR SETTINGS FOR 1948–54 MODELS

B.S.A. Model	Main Jet	Needle Jet	Throttle Valve	Needle Position
A7 (1948–50) . . .	140	0·107	6/3	3
A7 (1951–3) . . .	140	0·107	6/4	3
A7 Star Twin (1949–50) .	110	0·107	5/4	4
A7 Star Twin (1951–3) .	160	0·107	6/4	3
A7 Star Twin (1954) . .	350	0·109	6	4
A7 Shooting Star (1954) .	170	0·107	6/4	3
A10 Golden Flash (1950–3)	170	0·108	6/4	2
A10 Golden Flash (1954) .	170	0·107	6/4	2
A10 Road Rocket (1954) .	340	0·109	6	4

Pilot Jet and Throttle-stop Adjustment. A combined adjustment should be made with the *engine warm*. Start up the engine and close the throttle twist-grip. Open the air lever fully and advance the ignition lever (where fitted) as far as is practicable to obtain a smooth tick-over.

Loosen the lock-nut (omitted on the "Monobloc" type carburettor) which secures the throttle-stop screw, and *screw in* the pilot-air adjusting screw until the mixture is excessively rich and the engine commences to run unevenly. Now weaken the mixture by *unscrewing* the pilot-air adjusting screw until the engine runs evenly. Avoid excessive weakening of the mixture which would probably cause the engine to spit back through the carburettor or even stop when the throttle is opened. With the pilot-air adjusting screw properly set, it may be found that the engine is running excessively fast. In this case unscrew the throttle-stop until the engine runs at an even and steady tick-over.

Where a considerable throttle-stop adjustment has to be made, further adjustment of the pilot-air adjusting screw may be required in order to obtain a perfect slow-running mixture.

Do not make the combined adjustment so that the engine ticks-over very slowly. This has an adverse effect on oil circulation and can cause low-temperature condensation of fuel in the cylinders. Neither are good for

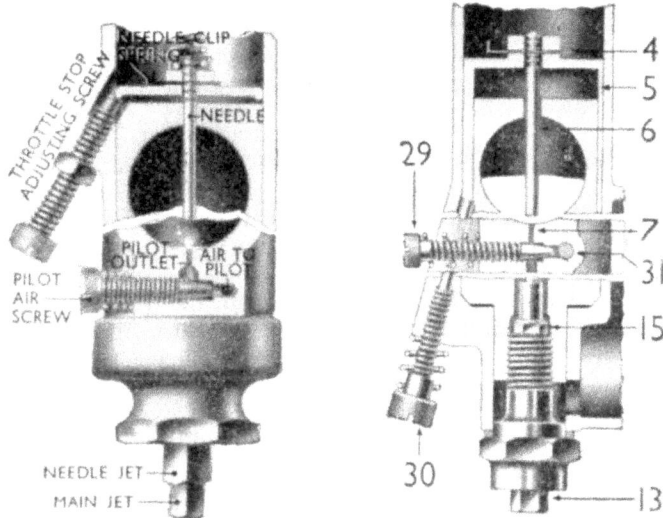

Fig. 9. Showing Throttle-stop and Pilot-air Adjusting Screws on (left) the Amal Standard-type Carburettor and (right) the "Monobloc" type Carburettor

A "monobloc" type instrument is fitted to all 1955–62 vertical twins with "swinging arm" rear suspension.

the engine. Also avoid allowing the engine to tick-over fast. This can cause over-heating. The ill effects of running on an excessively rich or weak mixture are considerable.

Aim at obtaining the best tick-over on a mixture just *approaching* the weak side. When really satisfactory slow-running* has been obtained tighten the lock-nut (standard-type carburettor) on the throttle-stop screw without disturbing the position of the screw.

* Rev the engine up and down sharply several times (while at rest and while riding) and note whether the engine exhaust is nice and crisp, with no "flat spots" or "spitting-back" occurring as the twist-grip is turned. It is essential to combine good tick-over with good and smooth acceleration.

The Jet-needle Position. If the petrol consumption of a vertical twin increases after a big mileage, in spite of the general condition of the engine being good, try the effect of *lowering* the tapered jet-needle, attached to the throttle valve, by one groove, and leave it in the position where the best performance and petrol consumption are obtained. Some wear of the needle-jet sometimes occurs, and in this instance a new jet is obviously required to restore good performance and economical running.

Wear of the jet needle (made of stainless steel) does not occur even after a big mileage. Where a marked increase in petrol consumption develops, always taken into account various possible factors such as worn cylinder bores, piston rings, etc. But scrutinize the carburettor carefully after stripping it down.

Obstruction in Pilot Jet. If the previously-described adjustment of the pilot-air adjusting screw and the throttle-stop screw does not obtain the desired result, and the engine will not tick-over quietly with the throttle almost closed, the air lever wide open, and the ignition lever (where fitted) advanced as far as possible, it is possible that there is some obstruction in the pilot jet. On the standard-type carburettor the pilot jet comprises a very small duct drilled in the jet block, and this duct can readily become choked if impurities collect in the carburettor float chamber. On the "monobloc" type carburettor a detachable pilot jet is provided, and this can readily be removed for thorough cleaning.

To gain access to the pilot jet on the standard-type Amal carburettor (*see* Fig. 7), remove the jet plug Q and the float chamber R, and then detach the jet block F by pushing it out of the mixing chamber A. The pilot jet J can then be cleared by blowing through it or by using a *very* fine strand of wire. With the "monobloc"-type carburettor (*see* Fig. 8), remove the pilot-jet cover nut and unscrew the pilot jet 16. The jet can then be thoroughly cleaned with petrol and blown through. Also make sure that the pilot outlet and the pilot by-pass are quite clear.

Indifferent Slow-running. If the pilot jet is quite clean and a careful combined adjustment of the pilot-air adjusting screw and throttle-stop screw (*see* page 26) fails to secure good slow-running, it is probable that the carburettor itself is not to blame for indifferent running at low engine revolutions. It is possible that there is an ignition defect or the mixture is being weakened by air leaks at a badly fitting carburettor flange, by excessive slackness between inlet valves and guides, or by badly seating exhaust valves.

It is occasionally found, generally on 650 c.c. A10 models, that one cylinder gets a slightly weaker mixture than does the other one. The result is irregular slow running and perhaps slight misfiring at lower speeds and small throttle openings, or possibly only on full throttle. The chrome finish on one exhaust pipe may discolour more quickly than on the other pipe. What is known as "induction bias"* gives rise to such symptoms, and in a genuine case of induction bias the only affective remedy (after investigating all other possible causes) is to fit a bias washer (*see* Fig. 10) between the carburettor flange and the manifold flange. The washer (Part No. 67-359) must be fitted so that its flange (and thin washer) is towards the engine and the *thicker* side on the side (l.h. or r.h.) where the weaker mixture is occurring. Fitting this bias washer causes the carburettor to be

FIG. 10. SPECIAL WASHER FOR CURING INDUCTION BIAS

This induction bias washer can if necessary be fitted to the inlet-manifold face to cure unequal distribution of carburettor mixture to the two cylinders (*see text*).

inclined horizontally slightly to the right or left, according to which inclination is required to direct more mixture to the weaker cylinder.

Poor slow-running is more often caused by some defect in the ignition system. For instance, the sparking plug may be dirty or oily; perhaps its electrode points may be set too far apart. Possibly the contact-breaker needs some attention or (if an ignition lever is fitted) the spark may be excessively advanced. Examine the magneto slip-ring for oil or brush dust, and see that both pick-up brushes are in good condition and bedding down properly. Also inspect both h.t. leads for defective insulation causing shorting.

Tuning Twin Carburettor. Where twin standard-type carburettors are fitted (i.e., on 1949–50 Model A7 Star Twins) the slow-running adjustment d escribed on page 26 for single standard-type carburettors applies, but the following three points must also be noted—

1. Should the engine fail to respond immediately after throttling up

* Induction bias is a characteristic phenomenon affecting certain vertical-twin engines having a single carburettor, but it is not common, has rather variable symptoms, and sometimes has effects so slight as to pass almost unnoticed. The basic cause is lack of identical running conditions in both cylinders, even though dimensions and method of manufacture are identical; it is, in fact, a little mysterious.

from tick-over speed, the "flat spot" which occurs on opening the throttle may be caused by one or both throttle valves, and/or needle-jets being worn. If careful inspection reveals that wear has occurred, effect the necessary renewals before attempting to adjust the carburettor.

2. Adjust each carburettor individually for its corresponding cylinder. Detach the h.t. lead from the off-side sparking plug and run the engine on the near-side cylinder only. Adjust the throttle-stop screw and the pilot-air adjusting screw on the *near-side* carburettor. Switch off the ignition, remove the h.t. lead from the near-side sparking plug, and reconnect the h.t. lead to the off-side sparking plug. Start up the engine on the off-side cylinder only, and set the carburettor throttle-stop screw and pilot-air adjusting screw in the same manner as for the near-side carburettor.

Again switch off the ignition, replace both h.t. leads, and then start up the engine so that it fires on both cylinders. An increase in tick-over speed may occur. If this is so, unscrew very slightly both throttle-stop screws, being careful to lower both throttle valves exactly the same amount, to ensure an even tick-over.

3. When you have obtained even slow-running with both throttle-valves resting on their throttle-stop screws and the twist-grip fully closed, take up any backlash in the throttle twist-grip control cables by making a very close adjustment of the two cable adjusters provided near the handle-bar ends of the control cables. This close adjustment is essential to ensure that *both* throttle slides *open exactly the same amount* when the twist-grip is turned inwards.

Excessive Petrol Consumption. Should excessive petrol consumption occur in spite of careful adjustment of the carburettor or carburettors, it is possible that one or more of the following causes is responsible for wastage of the precious fuel: late ignition timing (on models with an ignition lever); poor engine compression caused by worn or scored cylinder barrels, badly fitting piston-rings, or poor valve seatings; air leakage at the carburettor flange (*see* page 34); weak valve springs; carburettor "flooding" caused by a faulty float or needle valve (*see* Fig. 11); loose petrol-pipe union nuts, a faulty petrol tap, or slight leakage at one of the petrol-tank seams.

CARBURETTOR MAINTENANCE (STANDARD AND "MONOBLOC" TYPES)

To ensure continuous good functioning of the carburettor it is desirable occasionally (at least every six months) to remove the carburettor from the engine, strip it down completely, and thoroughly clean and inspect the components.

Dismantling Standard-Type Amal Carburettor. First close both petrol taps and disconnect the twin petrol pipes by releasing the single union situated at the base of the float chamber. Referring to Fig. 7, loosen (but do not actually remove) the jet plug *Q*. Slacken the mixing chamber union-nut *E*.

Unscrew the mixing-chamber knurled lock-ring *Z* (held by the spring *Z*1) at the top of the carburettor, and also unscrew the two bolts securing the carburettor flange to the induction-manifold face. The body of the carburettor can now be removed, together with the float chamber *R*, from

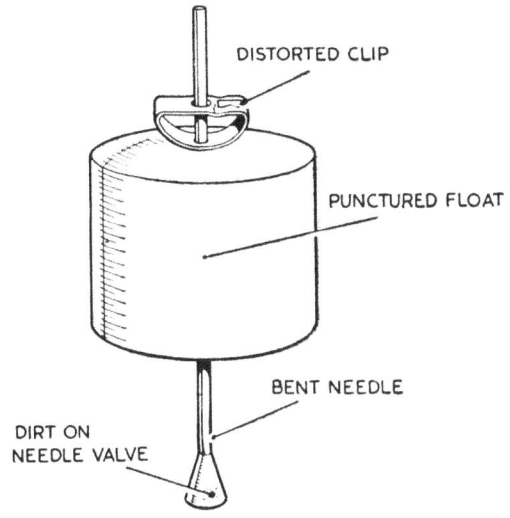

Fig. 11. Possible Causes of Persistent "Flooding"
Applies only to the standard-type Amal carburettor.

the engine. If a Vokes-type air cleaner is fitted, slide the carburettor off sideways and disconnect the rubber sleeve at its junction with the carburettor air-intake stub.

While removing the body of the carburettor, pull the air valve *D* and the throttle valve *B* (complete with jet needle *C*) from the mixing chamber *A*; temporarily tie up both the carburettor slides out of the way. It is not necessary to remove the air and throttle slides from their control cables unless it is desired to renew the slides or control cables. The jet needle can be adjusted for position if required, or removed from the throttle valve by removing the spring clip from the top of the slide.

Carefully remove: the carburettor flange joint-washer, the drip-shield, and the second joint-washer. If in any way damaged, the joint washers must be renewed before replacing the carburettor. Remove the bias washer also, where fitted (*see* page 29).

Now remove the jet plug *Q* and the float chamber *R*. Also remove the main jet *P* and the needle-jet *O*. Then completely unscrew the mixing chamber union-nut *E* and push the jet block *F* right out; if stiff, tap the block out gently with a wooden stump. Unscrew the float-chamber cover *W* after loosening its locking screw *X*. Then withdraw the float *T* by pinching the float-needle clip *V* inwards, and pull the float gently upwards.

Dismantling "Monobloc" Type Amal Carburettor. Close both petrol taps and disconnect the twin petrol pipes by undoing the banjo securing-bolt over the float chamber. Referring to Fig. 8, unscrew the mixing chamber knurled cap-ring 25 (held by the retaining spring 1) at the top of the carburettor, and also unscrew the two bolts which secure the carburettor flange to the induction-manifold face.

The body of the carburettor 20, together with the integral float chamber 12, can now be removed from the engine; the air and throttle valves can be removed during carburettor removal. If a C. & W. air cleaner is fitted to a model with "swinging arm" rear suspension, slide the carburettor off sideways and disconnect the rubber sleeve for the air cleaner at its junction with the carburettor air-intake stub.

While removing the carburettor, pull the air valve 2 and the throttle valve 23, with return spring, from the mixing chamber, and tie up the slides temporarily out of the way. It is rarely necessary to actually remove the two slides from the control cables. Renew the carburettor-flange washers if damaged, and be careful not to damage the bias washer if fitted.

Further dismantling of the carburettor is quite straightforward. To remove the jet needle 22, withdraw the jet-needle clip 3 on top of the throttle valve 23, and remove the needle itself. To obtain access to the float 9, remove the three screws 10 securing the float-chamber cover 11. Lift out the hinged float 9 and withdraw the moulded-nylon needle 8. Lay both aside for cleaning and inspection. The float-chamber vent, by the way, is embodied in the tickler assembly 6, and the top-feed union houses a fine-gauze filter which is readily accessible for cleaning.

To remove the main jet 15, remove the main-jet cover and unscrew the main jet from the jet holder 14, which should also be unscrewed. Remove the jet block locating-screw 18 to the left of and slightly below the pilot-air adjusting screw 19. Then push or tap out the jet block 4 and fibre seal 21 through the large end of the body of the carburettor 20. To remove the pilot jet 16 it is only necessary to remove the pilot-jet cover nut and unscrew the jet.

Cleaning the Components. Wash all carburettor components thoroughly clean with petrol and blow through the various ducts and passages to make sure that they are quite clear. Avoid using a fluffy rag for drying purposes. Pay special attention to the small pilot-jet passage in the jet block on the standard-type carburettor, and the pilot by-pass on the standard and "monobloc" type instruments. See that all impurities inside the float chamber are removed. On the "monobloc" type carburettor

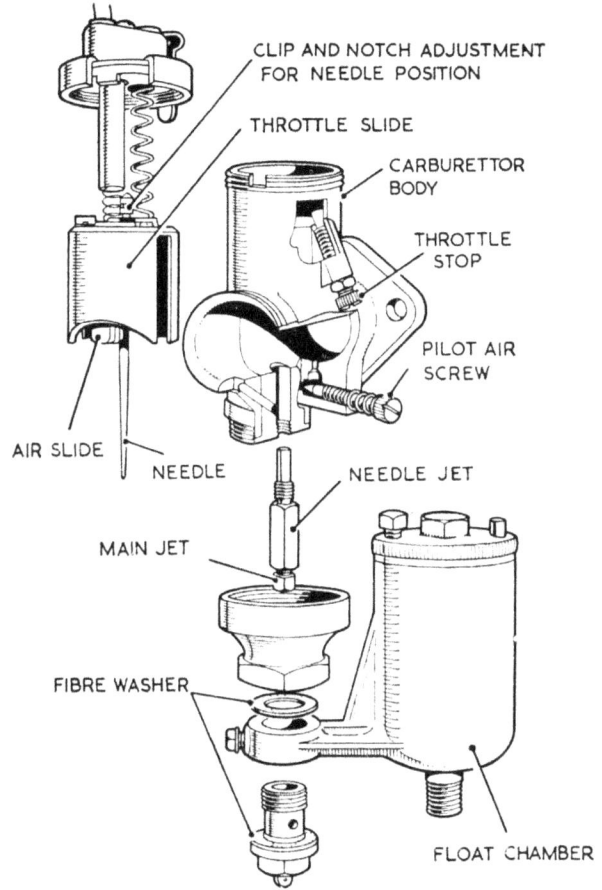

FIG. 12. THE STANDARD-TYPE AMAL CARBURETTOR PARTLY DISMANTLED 1948–54 MODELS

clean thoroughly the detachable pilot jet and remove and clean the circular gauze filter located inside the top-feed union for the float chamber.

Inspection of Carburettor. When dismantling the Amal carburettor it is advisable to make a close inspection of the various parts if the carburettor has been in continuous service for a considerable period.

I. THE FLOAT CHAMBER. Examine its components very carefully, and see that the air vent on the standard-type carburettor is unobstructed. The float must be in perfect condition. Clean the small moulded-nylon needle on the "monobloc" type carburettor very carefully, and be careful not to damage it. On the standard-type carburettor hand-polish the valve part of the float needle by rotating the needle on its seat while pulling it vertically upward. If a distinct shoulder is visible on the needle where it seats, renew the needle at once. Check for any sign of bending or distortion of the float-needle clip (see Fig. 11).

II. THE THROTTLE VALVE. Test this for fit in the mixing chamber. Should excessive play exist, it is advisable to renew the slide forthwith. See that the new throttle valve has the correct amount of cut-away.

III. THE JET-NEEDLE CLIP. The spring clip securing the tapered needle to the throttle valve must grip the needle firmly, and free rotation must *not* occur. Rotation causes the needle groove to wear. Always be careful to replace the needle with the clip in the correct groove (see Tables I *and* II).

IV. THE JET BLOCK. Before tapping this home into the mixing chamber, verify by blowing that the pilot-jet duct or ducts (standard-type carburettor) are clear and that the jet-block fibre seal (21, Fig. 8) is in good condition.

V. THE CARBURETTOR FLANGE. Examine this for truth with a straight-edge. Sometimes distortion occurs, and this can cause an air leak. If the flange face is slightly concave, have the face ground down on a grinder until it is dead flat and smooth. If you are skilled, you can use a file and emery-cloth for truing up. Examine the rubber "O" ring where fitted.

Assembling Standard-type Amal Carburettor. Referring to Fig. 7, refit the jet block F with a washer on its underside, and screw on lightly the mixing-chamber union nut E. Screw in the needle-jet O and the main jet P. Open the air lever almost fully and the throttle twist-grip half way; grasp the air slide between the thumb and the finger, and make sure that the jet needle enters the central hole in the adapter body H. Slightly turn the throttle valve B until it enters the barrel guide, when on pushing down the two valves, the air valve D should enter its guide. If not, slightly move the mixing-chamber cap Y, when the air valve will slide into position. Screw down fully the mixing-chamber knurled lock-ring Z.

See that the special bias washer (*see* Fig. 10), where required, is replaced on the induction-manifold face (with a thin washer interposed), fit the drip-shield, with a thin washer on each side, offer up the carburettor body, and secure its flange in position by tightening evenly the two securing bolts. Where an air filter is fitted, re-connect the rubber sleeve.

Replace the float T and float-needle valve U in the float chamber R, holding the needle against its seating with a pencil until the float and the float-needle clip V are slipped into position. See that the float-needle clip enters the needle groove. Then screw home the float-chamber cover W securely and lock in position by tightening the lock-screw X.

Insert the jet plug Q in the union nut E and very firmly tighten the union nut with a suitable spanner. Remove the jet plug and fit the float chamber and secure with the jet plug. Be sure that there is a fibre washer above and below the float-chamber lug as shown in Fig. 12. When the float chamber has been correctly positioned, tighten the jet plug firmly. Finally reconnect both petrol pipes and tighten the single union at the base of the float chamber. In the event of the pilot-air adjusting screw having been disturbed, adjust it and the throttle-stop screw as described on page 26.

Jet-needle Wear. The needle taper does *not* wear, though some wear of a groove may occur if the jet-needle clip is not grasping the needle firmly. Should the fuel mixture be too rich, it is possible that the needle-jet needs renewing because of wear. It is assumed that the carburettor is correctly adjusted and that no flooding occurs.

Assembling "Monobloc"-type Amal Carburettor. This should be done in the reverse order of dismantling and should present no special difficulty. Referring to Fig. 8, screw home the pilot jet 16 and the pilot-jet cover nut, not omitting to replace its washer. Push or tap home the jet block 4 and fibre washer 21 through the top end of the mixing-chamber body 20. See that the washer fitted to the stub of the jet block is in good condition. Then fit the jet block locating screw 18. Screw the needle-jet 13 into the jet holder 14 and screw the holder into the jet block, after checking that the washer for the holder is sound. Next screw the main jet 15 into the jet holder and replace the main-jet cover.

Replace the moulded-nylon float-needle 8 in the float chamber 12, and fit the hinged float 9 with the narrow side of the hinge uppermost. Afterwards fit the float-chamber cover 11 and secure by means of the three screws 10. Verify that the cover face, washer, and body face are absolutely clean and undamaged.

If previously removed, attach the jet needle 22 to the throttle valve 23 and secure with the jet-needle clip 3, making sure that the clip enters the correct groove (*see* Table I on page 26).

Position the carburettor-flange washers and the drip shield, and offer up the carburettor to the inlet-manifold flange, after easing the air and throttle valves 2, 23 down into the body of the carburettor 20. When easing the throttle valve home, make certain that the tapered jet-needle 22 really enters the centre hole in the jet block 4. If a C. & W. type air cleaner is fitted, slide the carburettor home and re-connect the rubber sleeve to the air-intake stub. Secure the carburettor flange firmly to the induction manifold by means of the two bolts, and then tighten the mixing-chamber knurled cap-ring 25. See that the throttle valve 23 works freely when this is firmly tightened down.

Finally reconnect the twin petrol pipes by tightening the banjo securing-bolt 7 over the float chamber 12.

THE AIR CLEANER

Air cleaners have been fitted to all 1948–59 500 c.c. and 650 c.c. B.S.A. vertical twins except the 1949–50 Model A7 Star Twins with dual carburettors, and on some of the sports models.

Two different types of large capacity air cleaners have been specified: the Vokes "Microvee" type and the C. & W. type. The former type is

FIG. 13. VOKES "MICROVEE" AIR CLEANER FITTED TO B.S.A. TWINS WITH PLUNGER-TYPE REAR SPRINGING

This cut-away view shows the filter element screwed to the back of the battery carrier. Models with "swinging arm" rear suspension have a C. & W. type air cleaner.

provided on models having plunger-type rear springing, and the latter type on machines having "swinging arm" rear suspension.

The Vokes Type. The Vokes "Microvee" air cleaner (*see* Fig. 13) is housed in the back of the battery carrier, and is connected to the air-intake stub of the Amal carburettor by a short rubber sleeve. About every 5,000 miles remove the filter element for cleaning.

To remove the filter element it is first necessary to remove the battery and the battery carrier. Disconnect the battery positive and negative leads at their connectors, after drawing back their protective rubber sleeves. Release the battery clamping strap and lift off the battery.

The battery carrier has a three-point attachment to the frame, one at the rear stay-tube beneath the saddle, and two at the saddle tube. Do not disconnect the rubber sleeve (connecting the air cleaner to the carburettor) from the battery carrier, but disconnect at the air-intake stub of the carburettor.

Now remove the three screws and carefully withdraw the filter element from the battery carrier. Fig. 14 shows the element withdrawn. It is somewhat fragile and therefore be very careful not to damage any part of it, especially the "convolutions."

Wash the filter element (*see* Fig. 14) very thoroughly in petrol, *dry it*, and then screw the element plate to the back of the battery carrier by means of

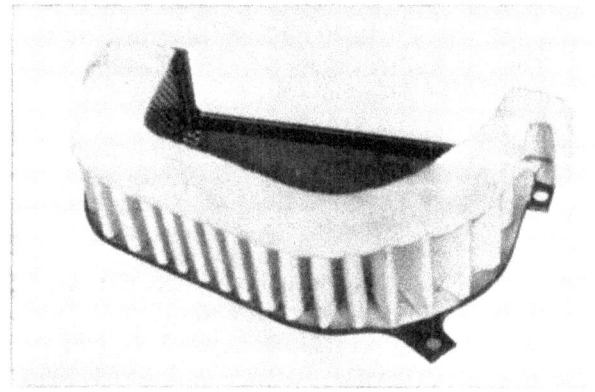

FIG. 14. VOKES "MICROVEE" FILTER ELEMENT REMOVED FROM THE BATTERY CARRIER

the three screws. Afterwards replace the battery carrier, reconnect the rubber sleeve to the air-intake stub, and fit the battery itself, after checking whether it requires topping-up (*see* page 44). See that the battery is held firmly by the battery clamping plate. Finally reconnect the battery positive and negative leads. Be sure that the correct lead is earthed and that the rubber protective sleeves are pulled well over the connectors.

The C. & W. Type. The C. & W. air cleaner, unlike the Vokes used on machines without "swinging arm" rear suspension, is of the "oil-dip" type and is mounted in front of the battery carrier. It also is connected to the air-intake stub of the Amal carburettor by a short rubber sleeve. About every 5,000 miles remove the filter element for cleaning and dipping in thin oil.

To remove the filter element, first free the air-cleaner cover by removing the two securing screws or bolts which pass through elongated slots; the lower screw or bolt secures the cover to the frame member below the saddle; the other one attaches the cover to the battery clamping strap. Disconnect the rubber sleeve connecting the air-cleaner cover to the air-intake stub of the carburettor; slip the sleeve off the cover and leave the other end undisturbed. Withdraw the cover sideways and then remove the filter element from it after prising out with a screwdriver the wire circlip or taking out the five retaining screws.

Wash the filter element very thoroughly in petrol, dry it, and then submerge completely in thin oil (about SAE 20) for a few minutes. Remove the element, allow all surplus oil to drain off, and afterwards secure the element to the air-cleaner cover by means of the circlip or five retaining screws or single screw. Then replace the cover on the machine, attaching it to the frame member below the saddle and to the battery strap by means of the two securing screws or bolts. Finally reconnect the rubber sleeve (from the carburettor air-intake) to the cover. Renewal of the filter element is advisable after a big mileage.

On Sports Models. Although a large capacity air cleaner is not fitted as standard on sports-type twins (e.g. "Shooting Star" and "Super Rocket"), a smaller capacity filter is fitted as an extra on some of these machines. Where a filter of this type is fitted the complete unit can be unscrewed from the carburettor air intake and the element itself removed after undoing a single screw. Its cleaning can be effected as previously described for the C. & W. type filter element.

TABLE III. CARBURETTOR SETTINGS FOR 1960–2 MODELS

B.S.A. Model	Main Jet	Pilot Jet	Throttle Valve	Needle Position
A7 Twin (1960–1)	210	25	$3\frac{1}{2}$	2
A7 Shooting Star (1960–1)	270	30	$3\frac{1}{2}$	3
A10 Golden Flash (1960–1)	250	30	$3\frac{1}{2}$	3
A10 Super Rocket (1960–2)	420	25	3	2

3 Care of Lighting System

ALL 1947–62 B.S.A. 500 c.c. and 650 c.c. O.H.V. vertical twins have Lucas electric lighting equipment and horns included in their standard specifications.

The Lucas lighting equipment comprises the following: a gear-driven type E3H or E3L dynamo mounted at the front of the crankcase between the engine plates; a compensated-voltage-control unit (regulator and cut-out) beneath the saddle or dualseat (in the tool-box on most "swinging arm" models); a 6-volt, 12 amp/h lead-acid type battery strapped to the battery carrier, or mounted beneath the dualseat on the "swinging arm" models; and various types of tail lamps and stop-tail lamps.

The Lucas Dynamos. The gear-driven E3H (1948–9) and E3L (1950–62) dynamos are both similar, but the former has a lubricator fitted to the commutator end-bracket (*see* Fig. 15) to enable occasional lubrication to be attended to. Each dynamo is of the two-brush type, and in conjunction with the compensated-voltage-control unit (fitted to all models having a Lucas dynamo) maintains automatic and compensated charging of the battery according to its state of charge and the load imposed upon it by the lamps, etc.

DYNAMO MAINTENANCE

Disconnecting the Battery. It is quite unnecessary to disconnect the positive lead* at the battery end when removing the commutator coverband, but always necessary to disconnect this lead when making any alterations or adjustments to the wiring circuit. To disconnect on some earlier models, push back the rubber shield and unscrew the cable connector; see that you do not make contact with the frame and short-circuit the battery. Pull the rubber shield well over the connector (where fitted) on reconnecting.

On later batteries with detachable cable-connectors, unscrew the knurled nut and withdraw the collet or cone-shaped insert. Observe that the collets for the positive and negative terminals are *not* interchangeable.

Note that should you at any time ride with the battery disconnected, or in any way out of service, it is permissible to turn the lighting switch to *any position* without endangering the equipment.

* The negative lead of the "positive earth" system is not used, i.e., on 1947–51 models.

The Commutator Brushes. Remove the metal cover-band from the commutator end-bracket about every 10,000 miles and examine the brush-gear (*see* Figs. 15 and 16) and also the commutator. Verify that the two brushes move freely in their holders by holding back each brush spring and gently pulling on the flexible connector. The brush should move without any sluggishness, and should return to its original position and make firm contact with the commutator immediately you release the flexible connector. Be careful when testing each brush to release the connector gently:

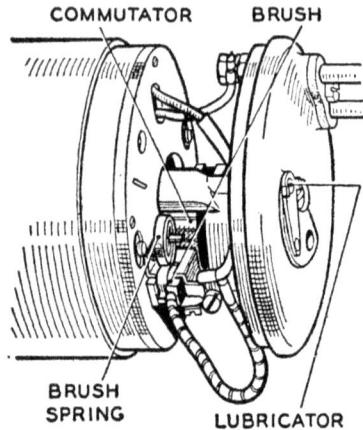

Fig. 15. Commutator End of Lucas E3H Dynamo

This type of dynamo is fitted to 1948–9 B.S.A. vertical twins and a few drops of high-grade thin machine oil should be inserted through the lubricator about every 1,000 miles.

make sure that the brush does not stick in its holder, otherwise there is some risk of the brush being damaged.

Carbon brushes in good condition should be quite clean and bed down over the whole of their contacting faces. Remove a sticking or dirty brush and clean it thoroughly with a cloth moistened with petrol. Afterwards make absolutely sure that each brush is replaced in its original position, i.e., in the correct holder. This ensures that the brush beds properly.

Brushes which after long service have become worn to the extent of $\frac{5}{16}$ in. in length require to be renewed. This should be done in the following manner: first release the eyelet on each brush lead by unscrewing the hexagonal nut or screw at the terminal; then withdraw the brush from its holder while holding back its spring lever out of the way. Always fit commutator brushes of genuine Lucas manufacture.

Inspect the brush springs occasionally to confirm that they have sufficient tension to keep the brushes pressed firmly against the commutator segments when the armature is rotating. This applies particularly where the brushes have been much used and a considerable shortening of the brushes has occurred.

When renewal of brushes or springs is called for, always use the correct type for the particular dynamo. It is advisable to have new brushes fitted by a Lucas service agent to ensure that the new brushes are properly bedded to the commutator.

Note that the metal cover-band on an earlier type E3L Lucas dynamo

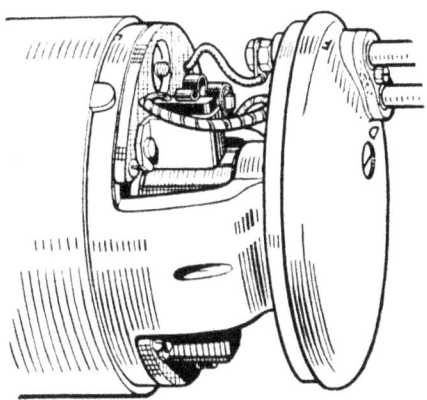

FIG. 16. COMMUTATOR END OF LUCAS E3L DYNAMO
This type of dynamo is fitted to 1950–62 B.S.A. vertical twins.

has a locating slot. This must coincide with a projection on the dynamo body when tightening the cover band.

The Commutator. The commutator segments should be clean, free from oil, grease, or dirt, and present a polished appearance. If for any reason oil or grease gets on the commutator, some sparking will probably take place and it is likely that carbon and copper dust will collect between the commutator segments and cause trouble.

The most convenient method of cleaning the commutator (without disconnecting any leads) is to remove one of the brushes and hold a dry duster against the commutator (with a suitable piece of wood) while slowly turning over the engine with the sparking plugs removed to overcome engine compression. Should the commutator be very dirty, moisten the duster with some petrol. A badly neglected commutator may need expert attention to restore the segments to normal condition (polished and dark bronze in colour).

Dynamo Lubrication. *See* pages 40 and 66.

Terminals on Dynamo. The positive terminal of the Lucas E3H or E3L dynamo used in conjunction with the C.V.C. unit is marked "D" and the shunt-field terminal "F" on the dynamo end-cover. To remove the cables, first loosen the central fixing screw on the terminal block and remove the clamping plate. Then remove the metal sleeves and cables from each terminal. To replace the cables, pass them through the clamping-plate holes with the metal sleeves positioned over the cables and the wire strands bent back over the sleeves. Then push the sleeves home into the terminals. Finally screw down the clamping plate with the central fixing screw.

No Fuses Provided. Simplicity is the key-note of the lighting system, and because of this no fuse is incorporated. Provided that the lighting harness is undamaged and all connexions are kept clean and tight, it is practically impossible for any excessive rise in current to occur and cause damage to the lighting system.

Servicing of Dynamo. It is a good plan about every 10,000–12,000 miles, or when undertaking a general overhaul, to submit the dynamo to a Lucas service depot for inspection, cleaning, and overhaul (including lubrication). Should any serious defect be revealed, a reconditioned dynamo in new condition can be obtained in exchange for the dynamo submitted for inspection.

Under the "factory exchange unit" scheme, a reconditioned C.V.C. unit can also be obtained where necessary. When a reconditioned dynamo is obtained, it is advisable at the same time to have the C.V.C. unit examined and if necessary adjusted. Note that in the London area the Lucas service depots are at Dordrecht Road, Acton Vale, W.3, and at 757–759 High Road, Leyton, E.10 (phone: SHE 3160 and LEY 3361).

Compensated Voltage Control. C.V.C. is specified on all 1948 and later B.S.A. vertical twins having Lucas dynamos. The Lucas control unit consists of the cut-out and voltage regulator (working on the trembler principle), neatly housed in a metal box attached to the mudguard below the saddle, or (on most "swinging arm" rear-suspension models) to the inside of the tool-box. The function of the C.V.C. unit is to maintain automatically the battery at the correct state of charge. The C.V.C. unit controls the dynamo output according to the state of charge of the battery and the load imposed upon it by the lamps and horn.

With the lighting switch in the "Off," "L," or "H" position, the dynamo generates a controlled output, thereby relieving the rider of all responsibility in the matter of battery charging. When the dynamo voltage rises to approximately 7·3 volts, the C.V.C. regulator commences to function. Note that while riding by day with a well-charged battery the dynamo gives only a trickle charge, and the ammeter needle may register only 1 or 2 amperes.

As soon as the lamps are switched on, the regulator increases the output of the dynamo. If you switch on the lamps after a long run with the battery voltage high, you will probably notice a temporary discharge reading of the ammeter; soon, however, the voltage falls, and the regulator responds, thus increasing the dynamo output until it balances the lamp load.

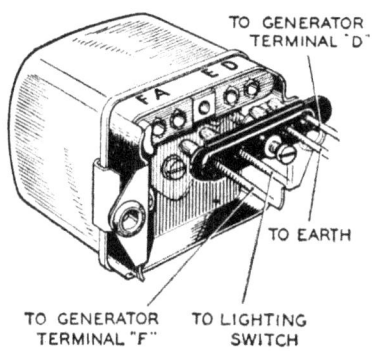

FIG. 17. COMPENSATED-VOLTAGE-CONTROL UNIT SHOWING CONNEXIONS (1954–62)

Note the sequence F,A,E,D. On 1948–53 B.S.A. vertical twins the connexions are in the sequence F,A,D,E, and two screws are provided to hold the connector plate.

The C.V.C. regulator increases the dynamo output when the battery is in a discharged condition and automatically restores the battery to its normal state of charge within the shortest possible period.

Maintenance of C.V.C. Unit. All C.V.C. units are sealed by the makers after being tested, and normally should require no further adjustment or attention. See that the connexions (*see* Fig. 17) are made correctly and are firm; also see that the cable insulation is sound. If making any adjustments to the wiring, first take the precaution of disconnecting the appropriate battery lead (*see* page 39). Be careful not to cross the dynamo positive and shunt-field leads, otherwise there is some risk of the C.V.C. contacts oxidizing or becoming welded together.

The Ammeter. Mounted on the headlamp or the headlamp cowl, the purpose of this instrument is to show the amount of current flowing into or from the battery. It is of the centre-zero type and is a guide to the proper functioning of the electrical equipment. For instance, if no charge is shown with the engine running and the lamps off, clearly the dynamo is for some reason failing to charge the battery.

CARE OF THE BATTERY (LEAD-ACID TYPE)

To ensure long battery life and the maximum illumination by the headlamp, it is essential to attend to the battery at regular intervals. The following are the essential maintenance points for the Lucas lead-acid battery—
 1. Always keep the battery well charged.
 2. Top-up the battery cells monthly with distilled water.
 3. Keep the electrolyte level with the tops of the separators.
 4. Occasionally test the condition of the battery by taking specific-gravity readings with a hydrometer.
 5. Keep the battery and terminals clean, and the terminals tight.
 6. If the battery is out of use, have it charged monthly.

Battery Charging. On all 1948 and later B.S.A. vertical twins the C.V.C. unit automatically controls current output according to the state of charge of the battery and the load imposed on it. In all three lighting-switch positions (*see* page 49) the battery is "on charge" while the engine is running.

Topping-up the Battery Cells. Every two weeks (more often in warm climates) check the level of the electrolyte in all three cells. On machines with "swinging arm" rear suspension it is first necessary to remove the dualseat to obtain access to the battery (*see* Fig. 18). To do this, remove the two bolts from under the rear of the dualseat and pull the latter backwards from the forward locating bar.

Owners of earlier rigid-frame models and models with plunger-type rear springing *must* remove the battery for topping-up, but this is not essential, though desirable, on "swinging arm" models. To remove the battery on models without "swinging arm" rear suspension, unscrew the clamping-screw and remove the screw and washer; then lift off the battery. On models with "swinging arm" rear suspension, remove the two small bolts securing the battery strap, disconnect the battery terminals, and lift off the battery.

Take off the battery lid and remove the three filler plugs. Blow through the vent hole in each plug to make sure that it is clear, because a choked vent causes an increase in pressure inside the cell through "gassing," and this may cause trouble.

With a clean rag wipe thoroughly the top of the battery, and afterwards destroy the rag. Check that the three rubber sealing-washers (where fitted) are undamaged and clean. Never hold a naked light close to the filler-plug holes, a most dangerous procedure.

If the level of the electrolyte in any cell is below the tops of the separators, or external blue line (1961–2), add distilled water (obtainable from chemists) as required to bring the level correct (*see* Fig. 19). The distilled water, by the way, is gradually lost by evaporation and must be replenished, otherwise the plates will become dry with disastrous consequences. Always top-up the battery just *before* a charge run, as the agitation while running, and some slight "gassing," will mix the solution thoroughly.

Where the battery, as shown in Fig. 19, does not incorporate an acid-level device (i.e., the PUW7E type battery used up to 1954), insert the

FIG. 18. THE DUALSEAT REMOVED TO EXPOSE THE LUCAS BATTERY

Applicable to 1954-62 "swinging arm" rear suspension models having the C.V.C. unit inside the toolbox.

(*By Courtesy of "Motor Cycle," London.*)

nozzle of a Lucas battery filler into each cell as shown in Fig. 21 until the nozzle rests on the separators. Keep the battery filler in this position until air bubbles cease to rise in the glass container. The cell should then be topped-up correctly as shown in Fig. 19. A Lucas battery filler is very helpful; it ensures that the correct electrolyte level is obtained automatically and prevents distilled water being spilled over the top of the battery.

When replenishing a Lucas battery filler with distilled water, be sure to replace the screw-on nozzle properly. Fit the rubber washer over the valve with the small peg in the centre of the valve engaging the hole in the projecting boss of the washer.

To top-up a 1955-60 Lucas battery having an acid-level device (*see* Fig. 20), pour distilled water round its flange (not down the tube) until no more drains through into the cell. This occurs when the level of the electrolyte reaches the bottom of the central tube and prevents further escape of air displaced by the topping-up water. Lift the tube slightly to permit the

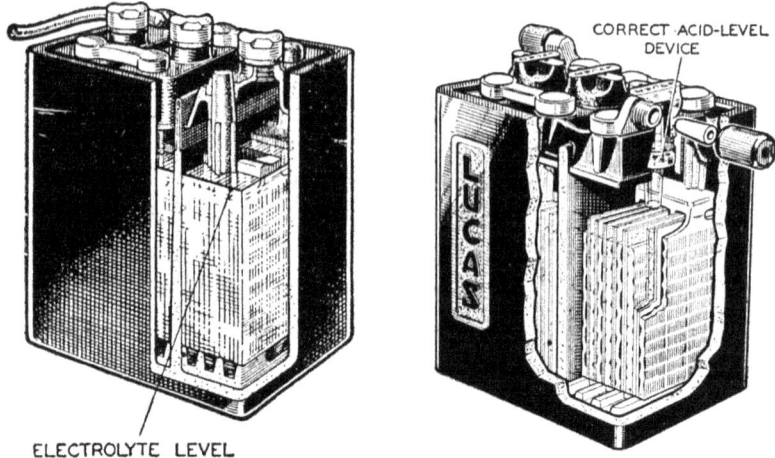

ELECTROLYTE LEVEL

FIGS. 19 AND 20. THE TWO TYPES OF LUCAS BATTERIES FITTED TO B.S.A. VERTICAL TWINS

The battery shown in the left-hand sketch has been standard equipment on 1948–54 models; that shown on the right is specified on 1955–60 models. Note the inclusion of an acid-level device. This is not provided on the Lucas MLZ9E battery fitted to 1961–2 models. The battery has a *blue line* on the side of its case to indicate the correct electrolyte level. Always top-up the battery to this level.

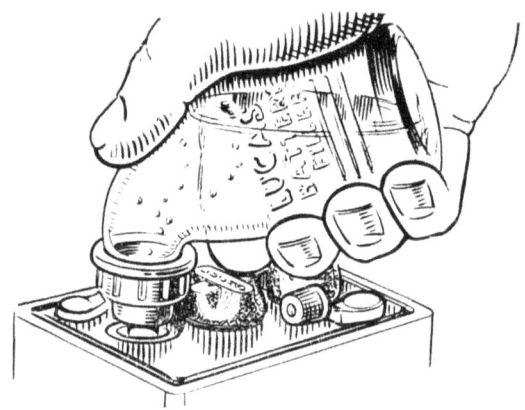

FIG. 21. USING LUCAS BATTERY FILLER FOR TOPPING-UP CELLS

small quantity of water in the flange to drain into the cell; the level of the electrolyte will then be correct. Alternatively remove the acid-level device and use a Lucas battery filler as previously described.

Do not add acid to the electrolyte unless some of the solution has been accidentally spilled. In this case add diluted sulphuric acid of specific gravity equal to that of the electrolyte in the cells. Finally replace the filler

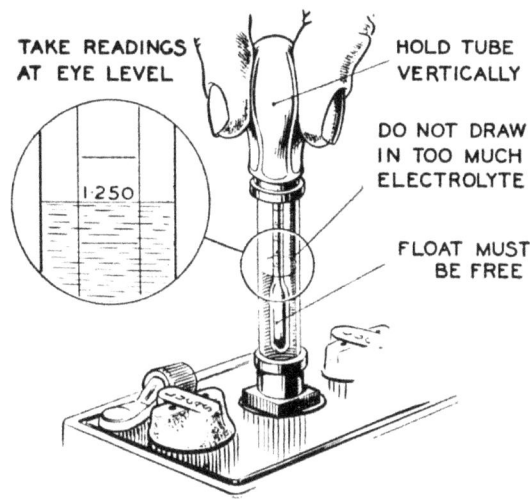

FIG. 22. CHECKING THE SPECIFIC GRAVITY OF THE ELECTROLYTE WITH A LUCAS HYDROMETER

plugs, wipe away any moisture from the top of the battery, replace the battery (if removed), and strap it down securely. See that the battery leads are firmly and correctly reconnected.

Checking Condition of Battery. Occasionally it is desirable to take specific gravity (S.G.) readings of the electrolyte in each cell. Use a Lucas hydrometer for this purpose as shown in Fig. 22, after returning from a ride when the solution is thoroughly mixed. An S.G. test is particularly advised if the condition of the battery is suspect, the battery is misbehaving or some loss of acid has occurred.

When checking the S.G. of the electrolyte in each cell, note that the spaces between the separators are not wide enough to allow the nozzle to be inserted. Therefore before taking a sample, tilt the battery to bring sufficient electrolyte above the separators.

The hydrometer contains a graduated float which indicates the specfiic gravity of the solution in the cell from which a sample has been taken. After taking and checking a sample, return the solution to the cell from which it was taken. Taking S.G. readings with a hydrometer is the most reliable method of checking the state of charge of a battery. If you have topped-up the battery with distilled water, do not take S.G. readings until you have ridden the machine and thereby ensured proper mixing of the electrolyte solution.

S.G. readings should be approximately the same for *all three cells*. If the S.G. reading for one particular cell differs substantially from the readings for the other cells, it is probable that some electrolyte has been spilled or has leaked from the cell, due possibly to a spill. Perhaps a short circuit has occurred between the battery plates: in this instance it would be necessary to return the battery to a Lucas service depot (*see* page 42) for careful examination.

Never allow the battery to remain for long in a discharged condition, or serious deterioration will almost certainly occur. After checking the S.G. readings of the electrolyte in the battery cells, wipe the top of the battery absolutely clean. Replace the three filler plugs and washers (where fitted), and refit the battery lid. Tighten the battery clamping screw or two bolts ("swinging arm" models) securing the battery strap, after making sure that the lid beds down properly; finally reconnect correctly (positive terminal earthed on 1952–62 models) the positive and negative battery leads (if previously disconnected). On a 1955–62 machine with "swinging arm" rear suspension, finally replace the dualseat.

Specific Gravity Readings. The S.G. readings for Lucas batteries used on B.S.A. vertical twins should be as shown in Table IV.

TABLE IV. CORRECT SPECIFIC GRAVITY READINGS

Temperature (Fahrenheit)	Battery Fully Charged	Battery Needs Charging
80°	1·285	1·235
60°	1·295	1·245
40°	1·305	1·255
20°	1·310	1·260

As previously mentioned, never allow the battery to remain in a discharged state for long, or it may be *permanently* damaged. A frequent cause of the battery being in a low state of charge is parking the motorcycle for prolonged periods with the lighting switch in the "L" position, unaccompanied by much daylight running. The remedy is, of course, to run more during the day and to keep the lighting switch in the "Off" position as much as possible until the battery regains its normal state of charge. Get the compensated-voltage-control unit checked up in the event of substantial overcharging occurring.

The Battery Connexions. Keep them clean, free from corrosion, and tight, otherwise the ammeter readings will *not* indicate the true state of charge of the battery. To prevent corrosion, smear the battery terminals with some petroleum jelly.

Storing the Battery. If you lay up your machine during the winter months, do not omit to give the battery a freshening charge about once a month at a radio dealers or a garage, otherwise permanent sulphation of the plates may set in and ruin the battery. Do not in any circumstances whatever drain the battery of the electrolyte, or permanent sulphation of the plates may occur and ruin the battery.

THE LUCAS LAMPS

Lighting Switch Positions. The lighting switch, mounted on a panel screwed to the top of the headlamp, or (on later models) on the headlamp cowl (*see* Fig. 23), has the following three positions—

OFF: Headlamp, tail lamp, speedometer light, and sidecar lamps (where fitted) switched off.

L: Headlamp pilot-bulb, tail lamp, speedometer light, and sidecar lamps (where fitted) switched on.

H: Headlamp focusing-type (1948–51) or pre-focus type (1952–62) main bulb, tail lamp, speedometer light, and sidecar lamps (where fitted) switched on.

As previously mentioned on page 42, battery charging occurs when the engine is running with the lighting switch turned to *any* of the three positions just mentioned.

Adjusting Position of Headlamp. Incorrect adjustment of the headlamp position spoils good illumination of the road and can much inconvenience other road users by dazzle. This fault can simply be avoided or rectified.

Stand your A7 or A10 B.S.A. model on *level* ground facing a light-coloured wall at a distance of 25-30 feet. Turn the lighting switch to the "H" position and observe whether the driving light beam from the headlamp main bulb is *parallel to the ground*.

Take vertical measurements from the centre of the headlamp glass, and from the centre of the illuminated circle on the wall, to the ground. Both dimensions should be the same. If the beam is clearly not parallel with the ground, slacken the headlamp securing bolts and tilt the headlamp upwards or downwards until a parallel beam is obtained. Be sure afterwards to retighten securely the two headlamp securing bolts, otherwise further tilting may occur through vibration.

Focusing Lucas MU42, SSU700P Type Headlamps (1948–51 Models).
Only on MU42, SSU700P-type headlamps is a focusing adjustment provided. As may be seen in Figs. 24 and 25 an adjustable bulb-holder secured by a clamping clip is the means whereby a focusing adjustment is effected when required. On all other Lucas headlamps fitted to B.S.A. vertical twins no focusing adjustment is needed or provided for the prefocus type main bulbs specified.

Adjust the focus of a Lucas headlamp fitted to a 1948–51 A7 or A10

FIG. 23. ON THE 1958–62 B.S.A. VERTICAL TWINS A NEAT HEADLAMP COWLING HOUSES THE LIGHTING SWITCH, AMMETER, SPEEDOMETER, AND HORN
(*By courtesy of "Motor Cycling"*)

model B.S.A. if the main driving beam is not uniform, is too wide, is of short range, or has a dark centre. Narrowly-converging and widely diverging beams give poor illumination and are liable to dazzle other road users.

To focus a Lucas MU42 or SSU700P type headlamp, release the spring fixing-catch or securing screw (*see* Figs. 24, 25) and withdraw the lamp-front assembly; then, with a screwdriver, loosen the screw on the clamping clip which secures the main-bulb holder. Then move the bulb holder forwards or backwards as required until the headlamp is correctly focused against a light-coloured wall 25–30 feet away. When correct focusing of the lamp is obtained, firmly retighten the clamping screw, and fit and

CARE OF LIGHTING SYSTEM 51

secure the lamp-front assembly. When doing this on a MU42 type headlamp (see Fig. 24), be sure to locate the *thinner* lip of the rubber bead between the reflector rim and the edge of the lamp body. On a SSU700P type headlamp (see Fig. 25) locate the metal tongue in the slot at the bottom of the lamp, press on the front, and fasten by tightening the securing screw. On some very early headlamps (about 1948) locate the top of the rim first.

Renewing Bulbs (1948–59 Models.) When fitting a new bulb to a Lucas headlamp, always be sure that the renewal bulb is of genuine Lucas manufacture. Bulbs are specially designed for use in conjunction with reflectors

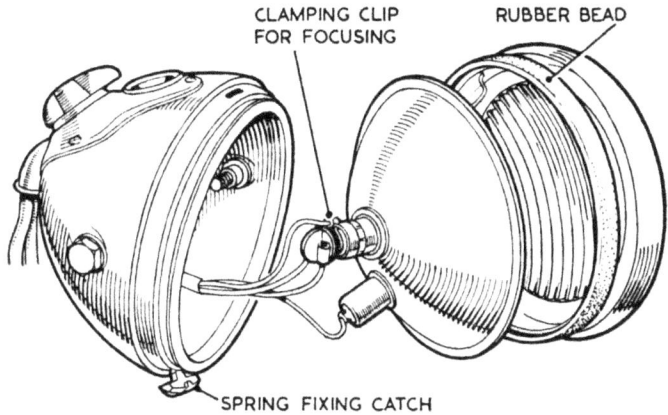

FIG. 24. LUCAS MU42 HEADLAMP PROVIDED WITH A FOCUSING ADJUSTMENT (1948)

Observe the clamping clip provided for focusing.

of the same make, and other proprietary bulbs will not necessarily give equally good results. All main double-filament bulbs, except those of the pre-focus type have a bayonet-type fixing, and the same applies to most pilot, tail, and stop-tail lamp bulbs. Obtaining access to the bulbs is very simple.

Where a focusing-type double-filament main bulb (as used on the MU42 and SSU700P headlamps) is concerned, always make absolutely certain that the bulb is fitted with the *dipped beam filament above the centre filament*. With the focusing-type headlamp it is also advisable to check the headlamp focus (see page 50) after fitting a new main bulb. A pre-focus type main bulb cannot, of course, be fitted incorrectly.

Correct Bulbs to Fit in Headlamps. The correct bulbs to fit in a 1948 focusing-type Lucas MU42 headlamp (see page 58) are as follows—
Main bulb: 6-volt, 24/24-watt, double-filament, SBC, Lucas No. 168.
Pilot bulb: 6-volt, 3-watt, single-filament, SCC, Lucas No. 200.

On 1949–51 focusing-type Lucas SSU700P headlamps the correct bulbs to fit are—
Main bulb: 6-volt, 30/30-watt, double-filament, Lucas No. 169.
Pilot bulb: 6-volt, 3-watt, single filament, Lucas No. 200.
When renewing a Lucas No. 169 bulb, always replace the new bulb with the dipped beam filament correctly positioned, as previously described.

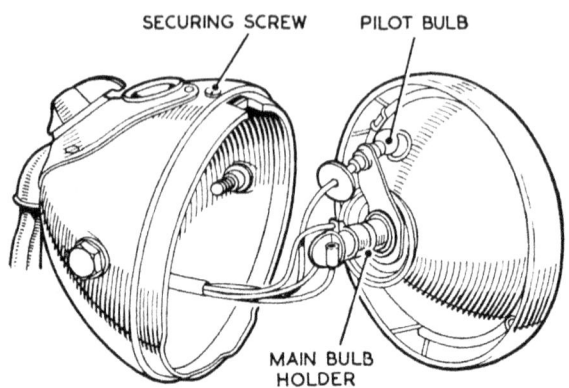

FIG. 25. LUCAS SSU700P HEADLAMP WITH FOCUSING ADJUSTMENT (1949–51)
The focusing adjustment is similar to that provided on the headlamp shown in Fig. 24.

To assist correct replacement, the metal cap is marked "TOP." The bulb holder (*see* Fig. 25) is secured in position by two spring-loaded pegs and can be readily removed from the rear of the Lucas reflector after detaching the lamp light-unit assembly.

For all 1952–62 Lucas headlamps of the pre-focus type (i.e., SS700P, SSU700P/1, MCF700P) the following are the correct bulbs to fit—
Main bulb: 6-volt, 30/24-watt, double-filament, Lucas No. 312.
Pilot bulb: 6-volt, 3-watt, single-filament, MCC, Lucas No. 988.

The Lucas No. 312 pre-focus bulb can be readily identified, as it has a broad locating flange on its cap. One fitting position only is possible, as the cap has a notch engaging with a projection inside the bulb holder (*see* Fig. 26). Referring to Fig. 25 or 26, to replace a pre-focus main bulb, turn the adapter *anti-clockwise*, pull it off, and remove the bulb from the holder in the rear of the reflector. Fit the new bulb in the bulb holder, engage the projections on the inside of the adapter with the slots in the holder, press on the adapter, and secure it by turning clockwise.

If the underslung pilot-bulb of a Lucas pre-focus SSU700P/1 headlamp needs renewal, slide out the metal carrier-plate above the pilot lens (*see* Fig. 27), and fit the new bulb (No. 988). Make sure that the carrier plate

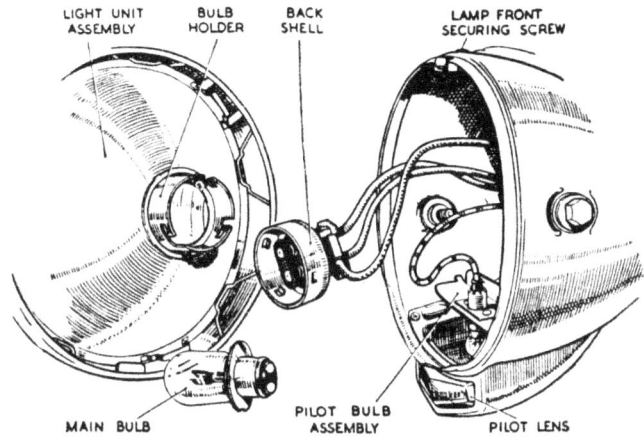

FIG. 26. LUCAS SSU700P/1 PRE-FOCUS HEADLAMP WITH UNDERSLUNG PILOT LIGHT (1952–4)
The light-unit assembly and main bulb are shown removed.

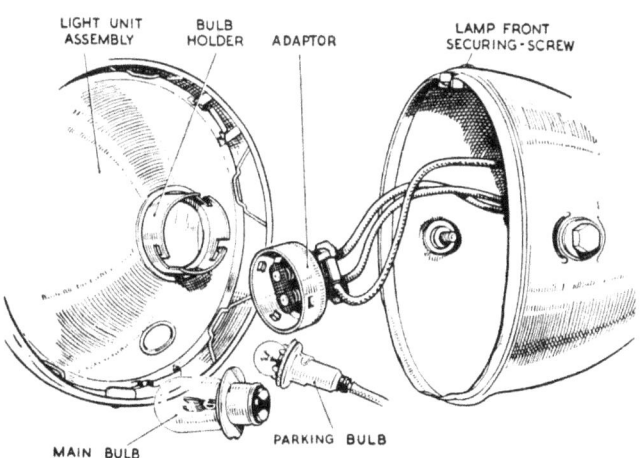

FIG. 27. LUCAS SS700P PRE-FOCUS HEADLAMP WITH LIGHT UNIT ASSEMBLY AND BULBS REMOVED (1955–7)

is pressed firmly home afterwards, otherwise it may work loose while riding and cause the pilot bulb to go out, possibly unnoticed by the rider. Those who dislike an underslung pilot-light (I do) are well catered for by various proprietary makes of "dual-lights," which can be readily fitted, one on each side of the headlamp.

Correct Bulbs for Lucas Tail Lamps and Stop-tail Lamps. The correct bulbs to fit in 1948–59 Lucas tail lamps and stop-tail lamps are as follows—

Tail lamps (types MT211, 490): 6-volt, 6-watt, single-filament, SCC, Lucas No. 205.

Stop-tail lamps (types 477-1, 525, 564): 6-volt, 6/18-watt, double-filament, SBC, Lucas No. 384. Note that the locating prongs of the bulb are off-set, so that it can be replaced in one position only.

Speedometer-light bulb: 6·5-volt, 1·8-watt (0·3 amp) MBC bulb.

Headlamp Maintenance. Clean all exposed black surfaces of the lamp body with a good car polish, and polish the chromium-plated rim with a chamois leather or a soft, dry cloth, after washing off any dirt with water.

To clean any reflector finger-marks (except on lamps with Lucas light-units), polish the surface gently with a chamois leather or with a clean *very soft* dry cloth such as a Selvyt. On cowled headlamps having a Lucas light-unit assembly and pre-focus main bulb the headlamp requires no maintenance other than to keep the contacts clean and tight. The reflector is sealed to the glass and in the event of either becoming damaged, the complete light unit assembly must be replaced.

THE ELECTRIC HORN

It is not normally desirable to make any adjustment to the electric horn (except perhaps very occasionally, for tone). The horn fitted to most B.S.A. vertical twins is the Lucas type HF1234. On a few horns of this type manufactured during 1950–1 no tone-adjustment was fitted, but on the other type HF1234 Lucas horns an adjustment screw is usually fitted as shown in Fig. 28.

Tone Adjustment. If the performance of a horn deteriorates (roughness of tone and loss of power), the following tone adjustment can be made. Depress the horn button and turn the adjustment screw (*see* Fig. 28) *anti-clockwise* until the horn just ceases to sound. Release the horn button and turn the adjustment screw *clockwise* for six notches (i.e., a quarter of a turn), when the original horn performance should be restored, provided that no serious fault exists. Should a further adjustment be needed, turn the screw *clockwise* one notch at a time.

If a Horn is Faulty. It is undoubtedly best to return the faulty horn to a Lucas service agent for careful inspection and overhaul. Do not forget,

CARE OF LIGHTING SYSTEM

however, that an uncertain horn action, resulting in a choking sound or complete failure to vibrate, does not necessarily imply that the horn itself is at fault. Possibly the wiring of the horn has become short-circuited, the battery is badly discharged, a connexion is loose, or the horn-button bracket makes bad electrical contact with the handlebars. The action of

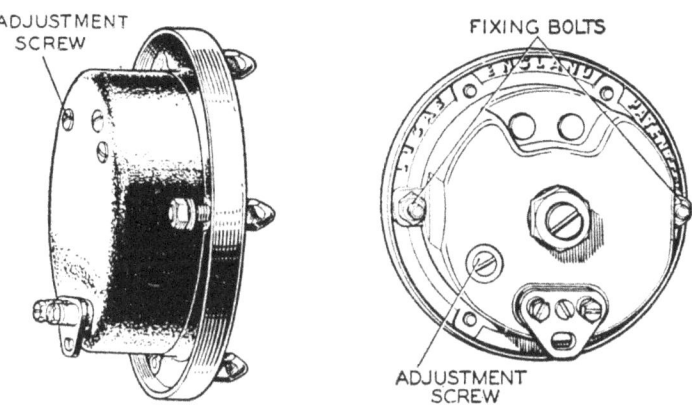

FIG. 28. REAR VIEW OF (LEFT) 1948–51 AND (RIGHT) 1952–62 LUCAS TYPE HF1234 ELECTRIC HORN SHOWING POSITION OF TONE ADJUSTMENT-SCREWS WHERE PROVIDED

the horn diaphragm can also be disturbed by the vibration of some component close to the horn.

WIRING OF THE EQUIPMENT

Before making any alteration to the wiring, or removing the lighting switch from the back of the Lucas headlamp, disconnect the negative lead (positive lead where a positive-earth system is not provided) at the battery to avoid any risk of short-circuiting. Two wiring diagrams are shown in Figs. 29–30. Reference to disconnecting the battery is given on page 39. The cables to the MU42, SS700P, SSU700P, and SSU700P/1 headlamps are taken direct to the lighting switch, incorporated with few exceptions, together with the ammeter, in a small panel which can be withdrawn after removing three screws.

Inspect the braided wiring-harness occasionally and see that no chafing of any of the leads is taking place. Tape up with insulation tape where necessary and make good use of rubber clips (obtainable from accessory firms).

The lighting cables can be readily identified by their coloured braided insulation, by coloured plastic insulation, or by coloured sleevings. The colour schemes used are shown in the accompanying wiring diagrams.

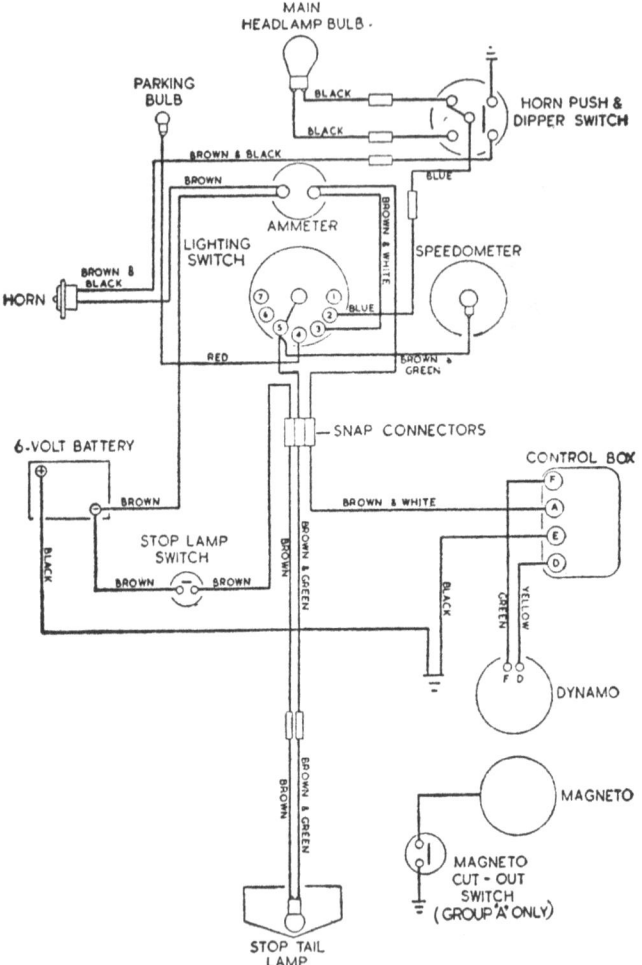

Fig. 29. Wiring Diagram for all 1955–62 A7 and A10 Models with Cowled Headlamps

Applies to machines with positive earth system, headlamp cowl, and "swinging arm" rear suspension. Does not apply to A10 "Super Rocket."

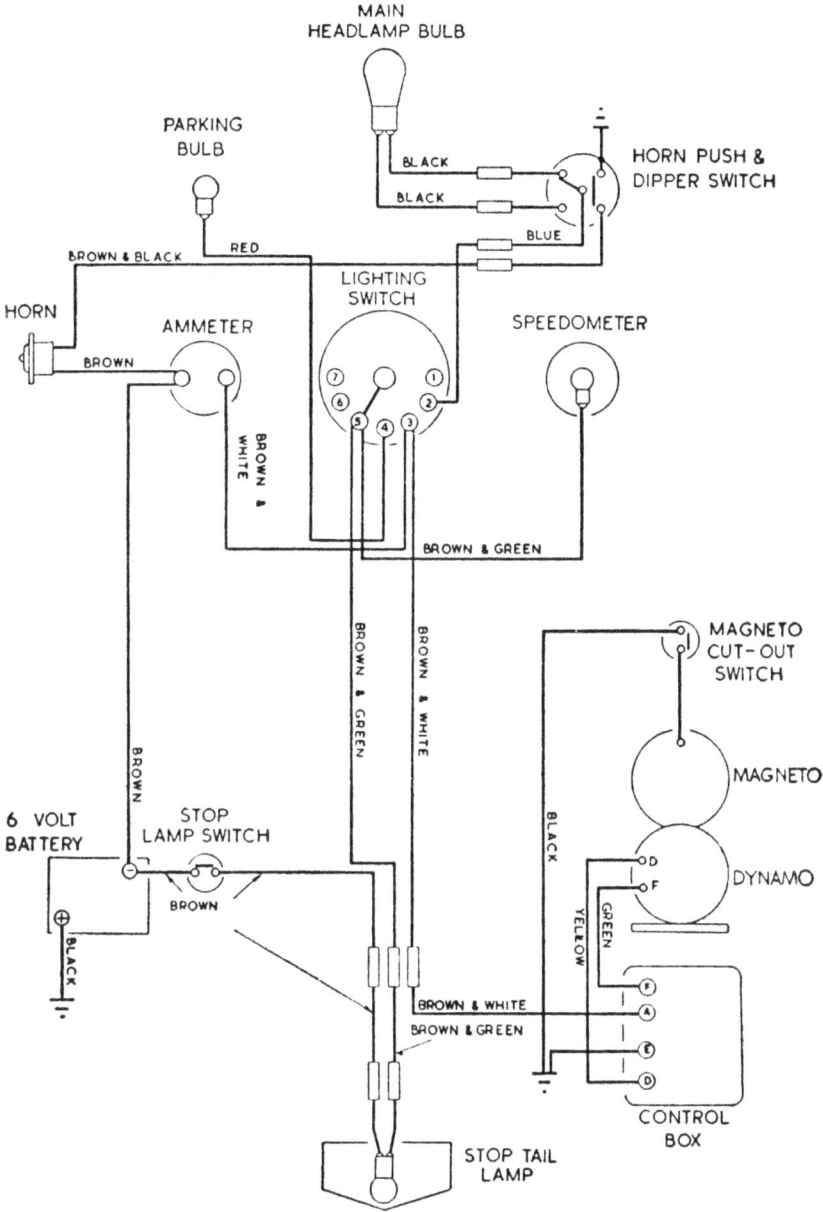

Fig. 30. Wiring Diagram for Model A10 Super Rocket
Applies to machines without headlamp cowl.

When making a connexion to the switch, bare about ¾ in. of the cable, twist the wire strands together, and turn back about ⅛ in. Remove the grub-screw from the appropriate terminal and insert the wire in the terminal post. Replace and tighten the grub-screw.

Note that the cables connected to the "D" and "F" terminals of the generator must *not* be reversed. To avoid this happening, the screw in the generator terminal block is off-centre and the screws which secure the generator terminal clamping-plate are not of the same size.

If Lamps Fail to Operate. If the failure involves only one bulb, renew the bulb immediately. Where the failure concerns all bulbs, check the state of charge of the battery. Should it be badly discharged, recharge the battery either by a long period of daylight running or from an independent source of charging. Make quite sure that there are no loose or broken connexions in the wiring system.

Bulb Wattage fo r Unlit Roads. Note that under new lighting regulation (introduced late in 1968) *all* motor-cycles having an engine capacity ove 250 c.c. must when ridden on *unlit* roads have a headlamp bulb main filament with a wattage of at least 30 watts, and a dipped beam filament of at least 24 watts. This means that if you ride a 1948 Model A7 with a Lucas MU42 headlamp (*see* page 51), its Lucas No. 168 bulb must be replaced by a suitable 30/24 watt bulb to comply with the new legal requirements.

4 Correct Lubrication

THE dry sump lubrication system provided on 1948–59 O.H.V. vertical-twin B.S.A. engines is highly efficient, and this chapter contains fully comprehensive instructions concerning the correct lubrication of all A7 and A10 type models. Very little attention is needed, but this minor attention is *vital*, and upon the proper care bestowed, depends first-rate performance and trouble-free riding.

Five Essential Points. In regard to the correct lubrication of the engine, whatever type it is, there are five essential points to remember. These are—
1. Always run-in a new or reconditioned engine with great care.
2. Keep sufficient oil in circulation.
3. Run on a good brand of oil of the correct grade.
4. Keep the oil clean.
5. Never allow oil dilution to occur.

Inspect Level of Oil in Tank Every 300 Miles. About every 300 miles, remove the oil tank filler-cap, inspect the oil level, and replenish the oil tank with suitable engine oil if necessary. The total capacity of the oil tank is 4–5½ pints. *Never allow the oil level to fall below the oil level mark on the outside of the oil tank.* When replenishing the oil tank, do not fill the tank more than about *one inch* below the top of the tank, otherwise some oil may seep from the filler cap. It would also render difficult the proper observance of oil flowing back from the engine into the tank. Fig. 31 shows a useful type of oil filler.

Running-in. Some general advice about running-in the engine during the first 1,000–1,500 miles is given on page 17, and observe these instructions carefully. The makers recommend the use of upper-cylinder lubricant (*see* page 8) during the running-in period. It is important during this period to keep the level of oil in the tank high and to change the oil regularly (*see* page 62).

Suitable Engine Oils. Always replenish the oil tank with a reputable brand of engine oil of the correct grade. The importance of this cannot be over-emphasized. Also make a point of buying oil only from sealed cans

or branded cabinets. Suitable engine oils for All B.S.A. vertical twins are—
Castrol XXL (XL during winter).
Shell X100–40 (30 during winter).
Mobiloil BB (A during winter).
Esso Motor Oil 40/50 (20W/30 during winter).
B.P. Energol SAE 40 (SAE 30 during winter).
Regent Havoline SAE 40 (SAE 30 during winter).

Warm-up Engine Gradually. Some riders, as soon as they have got an engine going, begin to race it, possibly with a view to impressing bystanders

FIG. 31. IT IS WORTH WHILE WHEN REPLENISHING THE OIL TANK TO USE A GOOD TYPE OF FILLER

Above is shown the Castrol type filler (a measure) in use. This prevents oil spilling over the tank, as often occurs when filling direct from an oil-tin.
(*By courtesy of C. C. Wakefield & Co., Ltd.*)

of the power of a B.S.A. vertical twin. This can cause hostility against motor-cyclists and for the reasons stated on page 17 is bad for the engine. Always warm up at a *moderate speed*.

To Check Oil Circulation. Periodically remove the oil tank filler-cap and observe whether the oil is visible, issuing from the return-pipe orifice in a series of drops. Immediately after starting up from cold the flow is more rapid, but this is because any excess oil which has drained into the sump is quickly transferred to the oil tank by the double-gear oil pump. In the rare event of no oil return-flow being visible inside the tank, stop the engine immediately, as most serious trouble is possible (*see* also note concerning the anti-syphon valve on page 65). Provided that a normal and regular oil-flow is observed from the return pipe orifice, you can safely assume that the lubrication system is functioning correctly.

THE DRY SUMP SYSTEM

How the System Functions. The lubrication system (*see* Fig. 34) on B.S.A. vertical twins is a modern dry-sump type and the "heart" of the

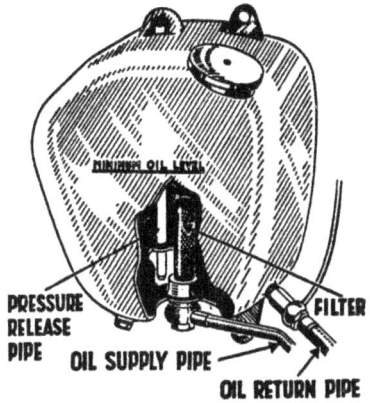

FIG. 32. OIL TANK DETAILS (1948–54)

This type of tank applies to all models with plunger-type rear springing. Note the vertical gauze-filter.

system is a double-gear type oil pump which is located in the bottom of the timing case. This pump pressure-feeds oil throughout the engine and then returns all surplus oil back into the oil tank.

On engines up to engine No. XA7-449 all oilways are internal except for the supply and return pipes from the oil tank. Subsequent engines have an external oil supply to the ends of the overhead rocker spindles from a by-pass pipe at the junction of the oil-return pipe to the oil tank (*see* Figs. 32, 33).

Oil is drawn from the oil tank through the wire-mesh filter shown in Figs. 32, 33 to the supply portion (with the smaller set of gears) of the gear-type pump, and this portion pressure-feeds the oil past a non-return valve to the timing-side main bearing and thence to the hollow crankshaft and the big-end bearings, while a further internal oilway supplies oil via a pressure-control valve to the timing gears and camshaft trough. The crankcase has a timed mechanical breather and anti-syphon valve.

After lubricating vital parts of the engine, and circulating through the engine in the form of mist, the oil drains down through a filter in the bottom of the crankcase, from where it is sucked by the return portion (larger set of gears) of the oil pump and delivered past an anti-syphon ball valve through the return pipe to the oil tank.

As regards the overhead valve gear, note that surplus oil from the rockers flows down the push-rod tunnel back into the crankcase.

Change Engine Oil and Drain Crankcase Every 2,000 Miles. About every 2,000 miles, preferably with the oil flowing freely after a run, drain off the whole of the engine oil in the oil tank. Prior to unscrewing the small drain plug on the off-side (1948–54 models), or the combined drain plug

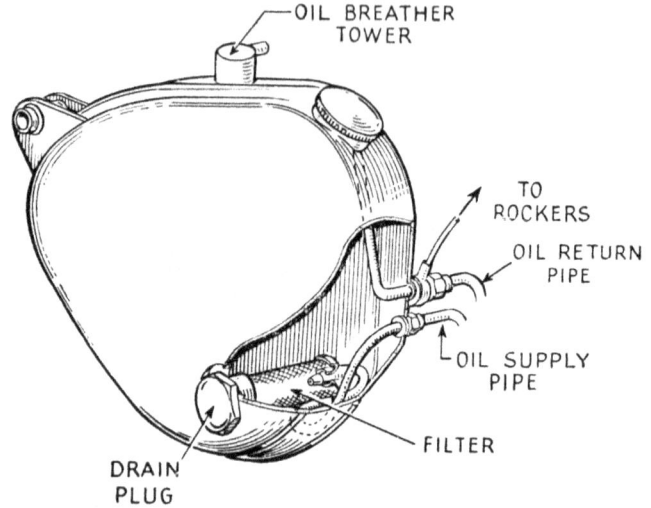

FIG. 33. OIL TANK DETAILS (1954–62)
Applicable to all (including some 1955) models with "swinging arm" rear suspension. Note the horizontal gauze-filter shown removed in Fig. 35

and filter (1955–62 models) it is wise to place a fairly large funnel beneath the drain-plug orifice and allow the oil to drain off into a receptacle large enough to hold just over half a gallon. When replacing the drain plug (*see* Figs. 32, 33) be sure to replace the fibre washer.

Wash out the oil tank with suitable flushing oil or thin machine oil. Paraffin or petrol should not be used for flushing purposes. Withdraw the gauze filter in the oil tank for thorough cleaning; also drain the crankcase and remove for cleaning the crankcase filter (*B*, Fig. 34). To drain oil from the crankcase, remove the small hexagon-headed drain plug, or alternatively remove the crankcase scavenge cover which is secured to the base of the crankcase by four nuts. These nuts must be loosened *evenly*. Removal of the scavenge cover gives access to the crankcase (oil-return) filter which comes away with the cover (*see* Fig. 36).

Having cleaned the oil tank and both filters, replenish the oil tank with

CORRECT LUBRICATION

the correct brand and grade of engine oil (*see* page 60). On a new Model A7 or A10 B.S.A. change the engine oil after the first 250 miles, and again

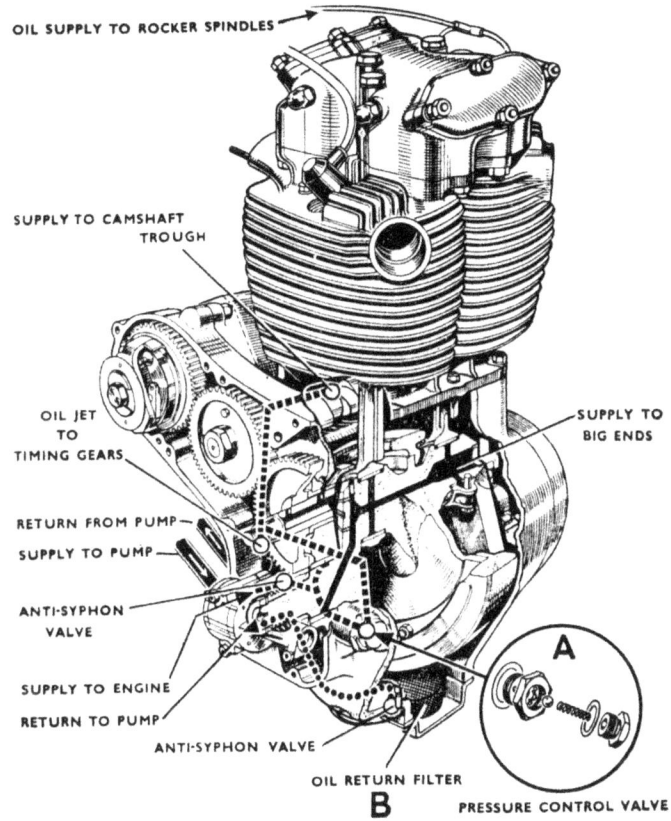

FIG. 34. CUT-AWAY VIEW OF VERTICAL-TWIN ENGINE SHOWING HOW THE OIL CIRCULATES

Applies to all 500 c.c. and 650 c.c. engines (*see* pages 61, 65).

at 1,000 miles. Subsequently change the engine oil and clean both filters at 2,000 mile intervals.

Removing and Cleaning Both Filters. To remove the vertical-type gauze filter from the 1948–54 oil tank *after draining the tank*, remove the oil-pipe banjo-union plug at the base of the oil tank and withdraw the cylindrical filter attached to the plug. Avoid bending the gauze when withdrawing the combined filter and plug.

To remove the horizontal-type gauze filter from the 1955–9 oil tank, it is unnecessary to unscrew the oil-pipe union, the filter itself (*see* Fig. 35) being attached to the large chromium-plated drain plug screwed into the off-side of the oil tank. When the unit is removed, the oil-supply pipe, which draws oil through the filter, becomes visible.

To remove the crankcase (oil-return) filter, unscrew evenly and in a diagonal order the four scavenge cover securing-nuts from the studs on the crankcase base, and lift away the scavenge cover and filter (shown in Fig. 36). Do not disturb the oil pump unnecessarily, as it rarely gives any trouble.

Wash both gauze filters thoroughly in petrol or paraffin, and dry them completely before replacement. When cleaning the filters, submerge them

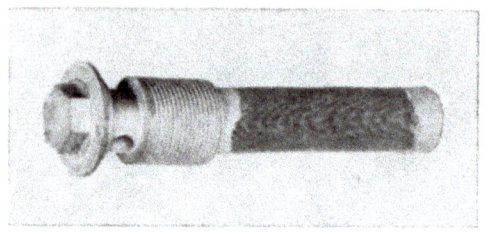

FIG. 35. COMBINED GAUZE FILTER AND DRAIN PLUG (1955–62)
This horizontal-type unit is screwed into the tank of all "swinging arm" models as shown in Fig. 33.

completely in a suitable receptacle. On no account use a rag for cleaning, otherwise some fluff may get caught in the gauze.

When replacing the scavenge cover (*see* Fig. 36) make sure that it is conveniently positioned and that the sump and cover faces are quite clean. Fit a new joint washer. Tighten the scavenge cover securing-nuts evenly and firmly to ensure an oil-tight joint. *Avoid excessive leverage*, or the studs may shear. Therefore do not use a *long* spanner.

Examining the Pressure-control Valve (All Engines). A pressure-control valve (*A*, Fig. 34) is located between the supply side of the double-gear oil pump and the big-end bearings. This valve is carefully pre-set to regulate the pressure of oil in the supply system. If the ball valve does not seat properly, the big-end bearings may be fed with insufficient oil and, needless to say, this can be most detrimental.

It is wise to examine the pressure-control valve periodically (preferably at approximately every 1,000 miles); verify that the valve is able to move freely and that it is not obstructed by any small foreign particles.

Remove the ball valve and thoroughly clean the ball and its seat. If the ball does not appear to bed down nicely on its seat, replace the ball and deliver a sharp tap on it with a light hammer and suitable punch; this should ensure good bedding down when the engine is running with the valve assembled. Before re-assembling the pressure-control valve, thoroughly rinse in petrol the various parts shown at *A* in Fig. 34. Note: it is most important that both hexagons are screwed right home and are firmly tightened.

Sticking Anti-syphon Valve (1951–62 Engines). On all except some pre-1951 vertical-twin engines an anti-syphon ball valve is fitted in the crankcase sump as shown in Fig. 34. Notice that should this ball valve stick in its seating, the return of oil to the oil tank will cease immediately. The remedy for this annoying trouble is to remove the scavenge cover (*see*

FIG. 36. SCAVENGE COVER AND CRANKCASE FILTER (1948–62)

It is important that the plate and filter are absolutely clean, and the washer sound before the unit is fitted to the base of the crankcase as shown at *B* in Fig. 34.

Fig. 36) from the crankcase, insert a piece of wire into the ball-valve orifice, and raise the ball until it is freed from its seating. Afterwards replace the scavenge cover and filter carefully (*see* page 64).

Excess Pressure in Oil Tank Pressure-release Pipe (1948–54 Models). On vertical twins not provided with "swinging arm" rear suspension, and having the type of oil tank shown in Fig. 32, some leakage of oil from the tank filler-cap sometimes occurs, especially when the tank is well topped-up. The cause is generally an obstruction in the pressure-release pipe creating excess pressure within the oil tank. The remedy is to insert a suitable length of flexible wire into the pipe at its lower end (just in front of the rear mudguard) and push the wire right up the pipe to clear any obstruction.

The Oil-breather Tower (1955–62 Models). On 1955–9 "swinging arm" models the oil tank has an oil-breather tower (*see* Fig. 33), and the foregoing instructions do not apply. See that the short length of tube which projects horizontally is kept quite clear of obstruction by occasionally inserting a very short length of wire.

Mechanical Breather in Crankcase. Note the remarks on page 67 concerning the cork washer which should always be renewed, unless perfect, when replacing the timing-case cover.

THE MAGNETO, DYNAMO, etc.

Lubrication of Lucas Magneto. Every 4,000–5,000 miles remove the contact-breaker cover. Then turn the engine slowly until the small hole in the cam ring (A, Fig. 43) is visible. You will observe that the hole in the lower edge of the cam ring is fitted with a wick which enables oil to reach the pad and cam face. Add a few drops of light machine oil, being most careful not to allow any oil to get on the contacts of the contact-breaker.

It is also advisable to lubricate the contact-breaker rocker-arm pivot, and this necessitates the removal of the complete contact-breaker. Remove the hexagon-headed screw from the centre of the contact-breaker and pull the contact-breaker off the tapered shaft to which it is fitted. Then push aside the rocker-arm retaining spring, prise the rocker arm off its bearing, and lightly smear the bearing with some clean engine oil. At the same time, also lightly smear some clean engine oil on the contact-breaker (carefully avoiding the contacts). When replacing the contact-breaker, be careful to ensure that the projecting key, on the tapered portion of the contact-breaker base, engages with the keyway cut in the magneto spindle, otherwise the ignition timing will be disturbed. Use *moderate* force when re-tightening the hexagon-headed screw.

On earlier vertical twins (about 1948–50) after removing the contact-breaker cover, remove the cam which is a sliding fit in its housing. Add a few drops of thin machine oil to the felt pad fitted in the cam housing. When re-fitting the cam, line up the location in the back edge of the cam with the pegs in the cam housing and push it right home.

Where manual ignition control (which includes a moveable cam ring) is provided, an extra pad is incorporated in the magneto housing and this pad should also be lubricated with a few drops of thin machine oil.

The Lucas Dynamo. Ball bearings are fitted to both the commutator and driving-end bracket, and these bearings are packed with grease during initial assembly. This should suffice until your vertical twin is stripped down for a general overhaul, when the dynamo should be taken or sent to a Lucas service depot for dismantling, cleaning, adjustment, and re-greasing (H.M.P. grease is required for the bearings).

On 1948–9 Lucas dynamos (of the E3H type) a few drops of thin machine oil should be inserted about every 1,000 miles through the lubricator shown in Fig. 15.

CORRECT LUBRICATION

The Cork Seal Between Dynamo and Timing Case. Whenever occasion is had to remove the dynamo, it is most important, when replacing it, to press the dynamo firmly against the back of the timing case to ensure an oil-tight joint by trapping the cork seal.

The Air Cleaner (Oil-dip Type). Appropriate instructions for dealing with the C. & W. oil-dip type air cleaner fitted to machines with "swinging arm" rear suspension are given on page 37.

THE MOTOR-CYCLE PARTS

Although it cannot be denied that the correct lubrication of the engine is of major importance, it is also true that correct lubrication of various motor-cycle components should never be neglected. Carelessness in this respect spoils the effect of a high power-output, and is also likely to accelerate wear and tear of the transmission and cause deterioration of miscellaneous parts. Fig. 37 shows a lubrication chart, and an appropriate key to this chart is given on the opposite page. If you observe the points summarized, you cannot go far wrong.

Types of Greases Recommended. Various motor-cycle parts which need regular greasing have convenient grease nipples provided, and a Tecalemit grease gun for the injection of grease is provided in the standard tool kit. Some motor-cycle parts, however, require to be lubricated with ordinary engine oil (*see* page 60) and oil caps or oil holes with protective spring covers are provided for the insertion of oil. Where grease is required, always use a recommended brand. B.S.A. Motor Cycles, Ltd. advise the use of one of the following reputable greases—

1. Castrolease LM.
2. Shell Retinax A.
3. Mobilgrease MP.
4. B.P. Energrease L2.
5. Esso Multi-purpose Grease H.
6. Regent Marfak Multi-purpose 2.

All of the above-mentioned greases are equally suitable and grease containers for quick filling of the grease gun are available; these eliminate the rather messy job of filling the grease gun by hand with a lath. For winter use, Castrolease Medium is suitable as an alternative to Castrolease LM (except for wheel hubs).

Note that after a long run in very wet weather the application of the grease gun to points normally requiring greasing is advantageous in that it is likely to force out any water which may have penetrated into the moving parts.

Lubricating the Primary Chain (1948–59 Models). On these vertical-twin models the primary chain runs completely enclosed in an aluminium oil-bath chain case (*see* Fig. 38). About every 2,000 miles unscrew the inspection-hole cap *C*, drain the case by removing the red drain screw *A* or vertical plug (on models with plunger-type rear springing). Then with the red level-indicator screw *B* removed, replenish the chain case with some clean engine oil (*see* page 60) to the level of the indicator-screw orifice. It is important to avoid over-filling the oil-bath chain case, otherwise there may be a tendency for clutch slip to occur. When checking the oil level

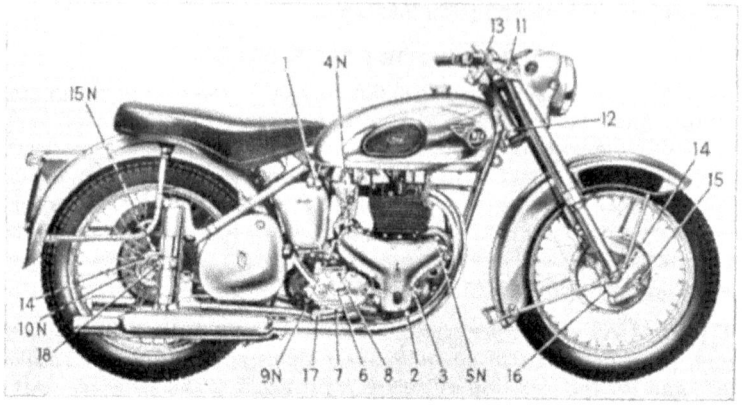

FIG. 37. LUBRICATION POINTS FOR 1948-59 B.S.A. TYPE A7 AND A10 O.H.V. VERTICAL TWINS

The lubrication points which are illustrated above apply to all 1948 and later models, except for a few slight differences. On some 1954 and almost all 1955-9 models the plunger-type rear springing shown is superseded by "swinging arm" rear suspension (*see page* 73). On pre-1951 models a rigid-type frame was specified and, except for the steering head, required no lubrication. No saddle-nose bolt (*see page* 73) is fitted to the machine shown. *Note*: the five item numbers followed by the letter N indicate lubrication points which are located on the *near-side* of the machine.

make sure that the motor-cycle is on level ground and not tilted backwards or forwards. See that screw *A* is replaced and firmly tightened.

About every 300 miles check the oil level in the oil-bath chain case and top-up where found necessary. The primary chain, unlike the secondary chain (not one having a chain enclosure like that shown in Fig. 69) does not become dirty, and it is therefore quite unnecessary to remove the chain regularly for cleaning with paraffin (*see* also page 74).

Lubrication of Four-speed Gearbox. The gearbox specified on all B.S.A. vertical twins is a big improvement on earlier types fitted to B.S.A. single-cylinder models, and it rarely gives trouble, provided that it is kept properly lubricated.

Referring to Fig. 61, page 109, about every 300 miles remove the two small screws securing the oval cover-plate for the clutch adjustment and the filler orifice (on the off-side). Also remove the level plug shown at *K*

CORRECT LUBRICATION 69

in Fig. 61. Then, if necessary, top-up the gearbox with the correct grade of engine oil (*see* page 60), until oil commences to trickle from the level-plug orifice. Allow all surplus oil to drain away and finally screw home firmly the oval cover-plate and the oil-level plug.

Key to Fig. 37

Item No.	Description	Lubrication, etc., Required	See Page
1	Oil tank	Every 300 miles check oil level and top-up as required. Every 2,000 miles change the oil and clean gauze filter	59, 62
2	Engine crankcase	Every 2,000 miles drain crankcase and clean crankcase filter	62–4
3	Pressure-control valve (crankcase)	Every 1,000 miles remove, examine, and clean	64
4N	Lucas magneto	Every 4,000–5,000 miles add a few drops of thin oil to the hole in the cam ring, or (on earlier models) the felt pad in the cam-ring housing. Also oil rocker-arm pivot and manual ignition control (where fitted)	66
5N	Lucas dynamo	Every 1,000 miles oil dynamo lubricator (where fitted). Have the ball bearings re-greased at a general overhaul	66
6	Gearbox filler	Every 300 miles remove cover-plate and check oil level. Top-up to the level of the separate level-plug hole	68
7	Gearbox drain-plug	Every 2,000 miles drain gearbox and replenish correctly with new engine oil	70
8	Clutch control-arm	Every 1,000 miles apply grease-gun to nipple provided	70
9N	Primary chain	Every 2,000 miles drain oil-bath chain case and replenish with new engine oil to the level of the indicator-screw orifice. Every 300 miles check oil level	67, 74
10N	Secondary chain	Every 500 miles apply grease or engine oil to the chain. Every 2,000 miles remove, clean, and grease the chain	70
11	Front forks	Replenish with suitable oil if excessive movement of the fork legs develops	72
12	Steering head	Every 1,000 miles grease the lower bearing with the grease-gun	71
13	Handlebar controls	Weekly oil control levers and exposed cables	72
14	Front and rear hubs	Every 1,000 miles apply grease-gun to hub nipples (where fitted)	71
15, 15N	Brake-cam spindles	Every 1,000 miles apply a few drops of oil or grease if nipple fitted	73
16	Front-brake cable	Weekly oil the ends of exposed part	71
17	Central stand	Every 1,000 miles apply grease-gun to nipple provided	74
18	Rear springing plunger	Every 500 miles apply grease-gun to both nipples	73

Remember occasionally (about every 1,000 miles) to inject a little grease through the nipple shown at F in Fig. 61. This nipple lubricates the clutch control-arm.

Draining the Gearbox. On a brand new machine it is advisable to drain the gearbox after covering 500 miles, and to repeat the operation regularly at 2,000-mile intervals. Draining is preferably done after a run when the oil is warm. Referring to Fig. 61, remove the drain plug shown at L, drain

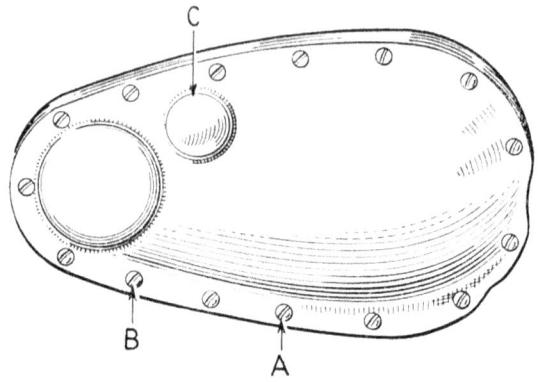

FIG. 38. THE OIL-BATH CHAIN CASE (1948–59 MODELS).
The correct total content of this chain case is 8 fluid ounces ($\frac{1}{2}$ pint). The drain screw, oil-level indicator screw, and inspection hole cap are shown at A, B, C respectively. Note that screws A and B have their heads painted *red* for easy identification.

the gearbox completely, flush it out with flushing oil, drain the gearbox again, replace the drain plug, and then replenish with engine oil (*see* page 60) to the level of the hole exposed by removing the level plug K. The capacity of the gearbox, by the way, is 14 fluid ounces (398 c.c.).

The Secondary Chain. Neglect of the secondary chain causes undue wear of the chain and the sprockets. It also tends to cause some harshness of the transmission. It is advisable about every 500 miles, or whenever the chain appears dry, to smear some graphite grease with a brush applied to the chain run. Alternatively engine oil can be used. The best method of lubricating the chain with engine oil is to apply an oil-can to the top of the lower chain run, while moving the chain by rotating the rear wheel.

When oiling the secondary chain see the the oil is falling upon the rollers, not on the ground. On later vertical twins provided with complete chain-case enclosure of the type shown in Fig. 69, in order to lubricate the secondary chain, remove the *front* rubber-plug and apply the oil-can through the inspection orifice.

Except on later models having the secondary chain enclosed as shown in Fig. 69, take off the chain about every 2,000 miles and submerge it in a bath of paraffin. By soaking the chain well, all dirt will be quickly and completely removed. Before replacing the chain, hang it up to dry thoroughly.

Before replacing a newly-cleaned chain on the sprockets, it is a good plan to immerse it in a tray containing warm graphited-grease; this type of grease will thoroughly permeate all the roller bearings. There is, in fact, no better treatment for a main driving chain, although regular greasing with a brush, or the periodical application of engine oil, will give quite satisfactory results. After graphited grease applied to a chain has been cooled off, wipe away all surplus grease. Note that the grease gets gradually squeezed out under load, and therefore at the end of 2,000 miles it is advisable to repeat the greasing procedure. Never allow the secondary chain to run dry for the reasons previously stated.

Clean the chain sprockets and, when replacing the secondary chain, be absolutely sure that the split end of the spring link faces *opposite to the direction of chain travel*. This is most important.

The Engine Shaft Shock-absorber. No lubrication attention is needed, as the unit is completely enclosed in the oil-bath chain case and automatically lubricated by oil thrown off the primary chain.

Front and Rear Hubs. On 1955-62 "swinging arm" models with full-width light-alloy hubs non-adjustable ball journal-type bearings are provided. These bearings are packed with grease during assembly and the only lubrication needed is re-packing of the bearings with grease during a complete overhaul.

On pre-1955 models having a grease nipple in the centre of each hub, apply the grease-gun about every 1,000 miles. If a sidecar outfit is concerned, do not forget the hub of the sidecar wheel. Three to four strokes with the grease-gun are sufficient. Avoid injecting excessive grease, otherwise some may get on the brake linings and reduce the efficiency of the brakes. Never use oil for lubricating the hubs.

On some earlier models (about 1950) an additional grease nipple is fitted to the off-side end of the front-wheel spindle. Its purpose is to lubricate the brake-drum ball thrust-bearings. Apply one shot of grease with the grease-gun, at intervals of 1,000 miles. Where a grease nipple is not provided, remove the front wheel very occasionally and fill the cavity in the splines adjacent to the brake drum with some grease.

The Steering Head. Every 1,000 miles lubricate the (lower) thrust ball bearing in the steering head. Give two to three strokes with the grease-gun applied to the nipple. Note also the hints on page 16 concerning lubrication of the steering-head locking device on 1955-62 vertical twins.

The B.S.A. Telescopic Front Forks. These are of very robust design and normally require no attention other than replenishment with fresh oil in the event of excessive up-and-down movement of the forks developing. Excessive movement, however, rarely occurs until after a very considerable mileage has been covered.

To replenish the B.S.A. forks, deal with each fork leg in the following manner. First remove the large hexagon-headed cap (and washer) shown

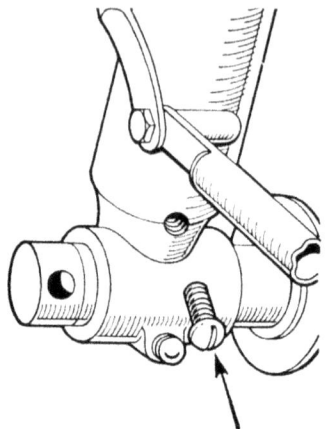

FIG. 39. SHOWING SMALL DRAIN PLUG ON TELESCOPIC FORK LEG

The arrow shows the screwed drain-plug removed from the fork leg.

at *A* in Fig. 79 from the top of the fork leg. Also with a screwdriver remove the small drain plug (*see* Fig. 39) from the lower end of the fork sliding-member and allow all oil to drain out. Complete draining is assisted by applying the front brake and depressing the forks a few times to drain out all surplus oil into a suitable receptacle. To ensure complete draining it is best to remove *both* drain plugs before making the above final effort. Such draining is recommended about every 10,000 miles.

To replenish each fork leg, replace the drain plug and tighten it firmly with a screwdriver. Then on 1948–54 models with plunger-type rear springing, replenish the fork leg with *four* fluid ounces (100 c.c.) of suitable oil. On 1955–62 models with "swinging arm" rear suspension, replenish the fork leg with $7\frac{1}{2}$ fluid ounces (213 c.c.) of suitable oil. Suitable oils are: Mobiloil Arctic, Castrolite, Shell X100-20, Esso Motor Oil 20W/30, Regent Havoline SAE 20W, and B.P. Energol SAE 20. A suitable glass-measure and small funnel can be obtained from a hardware store. Replace and tighten firmly the hexagon-headed caps.

Note that although no bad effects are caused by replenishing with slightly more oil than that stipulated above, do not exceed the specified amount by a large degree. Should the front-fork legs be filled right up, good suspension will cease and you will get "rough riding."

Handlebar Controls. It is a good plan, to ensure smooth action and prevent corrosion, to apply the oil-can weekly to all control cables where they are apt to bind on the control mechanism on the handlebars; tilt the bars so that oil runs into the cable casings. Oil all control levers and their nipples. When fitting new cables and casings, charge the latter with grease. A length of rubber tube can be used in conjunction with the grease-gun. Also oil all moveable control-rod joints.

The Speedometer Drive. No lubrication is necessary, as the drive enters the lower portion of the four-speed gearbox as shown in Fig. 61.

The Saddle-nose Bolt. Apply a few drops of oil weekly to the saddle-nose bolt on earlier machines fitted with a saddle. On all later models having a dualseat no lubrication is necessary.

Rear Springing (1948–54 Plunger Type). Each rear-fork leg has a single nipple (18, Fig. 37) for lubrication, and it is advisable to apply the grease-gun about every 500 miles. Give several strokes with the grease-gun. To prevent wear and rusting, a thin film of oil should always be noticed on the upper part of the chromium-plated telescopic member of the fork leg.

"Swinging Arm" Rear Suspension (1954 Onwards). The self-contained hydraulic dampers require no topping-up or lubrication, and the "swinging arm" pivots have "Silentbloc" bushes which do not require lubricating.

The Rear-brake Pedal. Weekly insert a few drops of oil in the lubricating hole for the rear-brake pedal shaft. Where a stop-tail lamp is provided, apply a *little* thin oil occasionally to the actuating plunger.

Brake Cross-over Shaft. On 1954–9 "swinging arm" models the cross-over shaft for the rear brake is liberally smeared with grease during assembly. After covering a considerable mileage it is advisable to remove the cross-over shaft, wipe it absolutely clean, and smear it with fresh grease (*see* page 67) prior to replacing the shaft.

Before you can remove the cross-over shaft you must first disconnect the rear-brake pedal and the cross-over shaft lever. Lower the pinch-bolts and pull the levers away from the shaft; note their respective positions to ensure correct re-assembly. Failure to do this can result in the levers being replaced incorrectly, causing inefficient functioning of the rear brake. Now pull the cross-over shaft out of the swinging arm.

The Brake Cam Spindles. Approximately every 1,000 miles apply a few drops of oil to the holes provided for oiling the brake cam spindles. Afterwards re-position the spring-clip cover over each hole. Note that 8 in. front brakes and all full-width light-alloy hubs have a grease nipple fitted; normally one shot of grease with the grease-gun is quite sufficient.

Front Brake. Do not forget during weekly oiling of the handlebar control-levers to oil lightly both ends of the exposed part of the control cable which runs parallel with the front-fork legs.

The Sidecar Chassis. About every 250 miles apply the grease-gun to the rear spring and shackle-link bolts. Follow closely the instructions issued by the makers.

Stands. Spring-up central stands are fitted to all except rigid-frame models, and a grease-nipple is provided for the grease-gun which should be applied every 1,000 miles. On earlier rigid-frame models having a rear stand, oil the fulcrum points.

Lubricating the Primary Chain (1960–2 Models). The oil-bath chain case (*see* Fig. 40) has a combined oil level and drain plug. About every

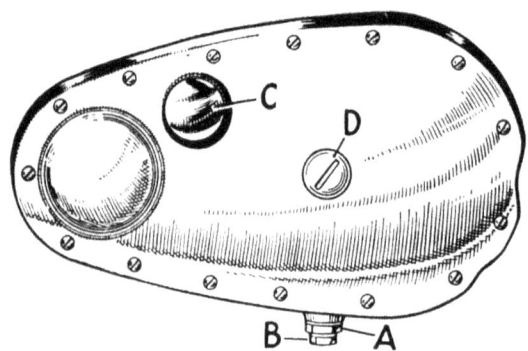

FIG. 40. THE OIL-BATH CHAIN CASE (1960–2 MODELS)

2,000 miles remove the drain plug *A* and allow all oil to drain out. Replace the plug and replenish the oil-bath with engine oil (*see* page 60) after removing the inspection cap *C* until oil begins to trickle out from the hole for screw *B*. Then replace screw *B*, and the inspection cap *C*. Check the oil level about every 300 miles.

5 General Maintenance

THIS chapter includes all essential information concerning the routine maintenance, dismantling, and assembling of 1948–62 B.S.A. type A7 and A10 vertical twins. To enable you to turn quickly to the particular instructions you need, it has been sub-divided into a number of main sections. All detailed references to carburation, the lighting system, and lubrication have been omitted, as these subjects have already been comprehensively dealt with in Chapters II to IV.

Attend to maintenance regularly and conscientiously, and do not wait until your mount "calls out" for attention.

Spares and Repairs. When you have occasion to forward or deliver any parts to the makers (B.S.A. Motor Cycles, Ltd., Service Dept., Birmingham, 11), or to an appointed B.S.A. dealer, do not forget to attach to each part a label bearing clearly your *full name and address*. To ensure prompt attention it is advisable to keep correspondence concerning technical advice and repairs on *separate sheets*. To facilitate identification of a part or unit, always quote the year of manufacture and the model (e.g., 1956 A7 Shooting Star), also the engine or frame number (*see* footnote on page 1), according to which is applicable.

Note that useful illustrated spares lists are obtainable from the makers or from appointed spares stockists. Widely distributed throughout the United Kingdom are numerous spares stockists who maintain a comprehensive stock of B.S.A. spares; some of them undertake general servicing and repair work. In the London area a very considerable number of spares stockists exist. Among those which have big stocks always available may be mentioned: Godfreys, Ltd.; Writers, Ltd.; West End Motors, Ltd.; Owen Bros; Elite Motors (Tooting), Ltd.; Cleare & Co., Ltd.; F. Parks & Sons, Ltd.; Eleanor Motors; Glanfield Lawrence; and Slocombes, Ltd.; also the big accessory firms mentioned below and marked with an asterisk.

Large General Accessory Firms. Nine large accessory firms (some of which have branches throughout the U.K.) handling general accessories, motor-cycle equipment, proprietary spares, tools, clothing, etc. are: Marble Arch Motor Supplies, Ltd.; The Halford Cycle Co., Ltd.; George Grose, Ltd.*; Turner's Stores*; James Grose, Ltd.*; Pride & Clarke, Ltd.*; Whitbys of Acton, Ltd.*; Claude Rye, Ltd*; and Kays of Ealing*.

Items Needed for Maintenance. You must have handy in the garage or lock-up some items besides the standard tool kit shown in Fig. 41. These

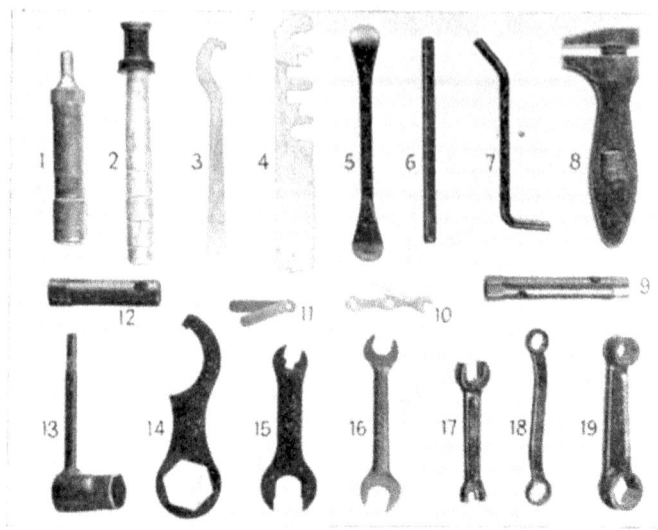

FIG. 41. TYPICAL STANDARD TOOL KIT FOR B.S.A. A7 AND A10 VERTICAL TWINS

On models with plunger-type rear springing instead of "swinging arm" rear suspension the spanner shown at 3 is, of course, omitted. There are slight tool variations for certain 1948–62 models.

1. Tecalemit grease gun
2. Valve grinding tool (suction type)
3. Spanner for adjusting rear-suspension units
4. Guide plate for assembly of push-rods and rocker-box
5. Tyre lever
6. Tommy bar (spring frame)
7. Tommy bar
8. Large adjustable spanner
9. Double-ended general-purpose box spanner
10. Lucas magneto spanner with feeler gauge
11. Tappet clearance gauge
12. Cylinder-head bolt box-spanner
13. Sparking-plug spanner and screwdriver
14. Spanner for telescopic-fork top caps
15. Carburettor and tappet spanner
16. Double-ended general purpose spanner
17. Four-way general purpose spanner
18. Ring spanner
19. Double-ended box spanner

tems include: a can of paraffin for cleaning purposes; a stiff brush for scouring dirt off the crankcase and underneath the motor-cycle; a tin of suitable engine oil (*see* page 60) for the engine and gearbox; a small funnel, or a proprietary oil-filler, for topping-up the oil tank and gearbox;

a canister of grease (*see* page 67) for replenishing the grease-gun; a large drip-tray for placing beneath the engine (also necessary when draining the oil tank, gearbox, and crankcase); a medium-size galvanized pail for washing parts with paraffin; some non-fluffy rags; a fairly broad, blunt screwdriver for chipping off carbon deposits; a tin of valve-grinding paste such as Richford's (coarse and fine); and a set of engine gaskets.

You should also have available: a pair of new gudgeon-pin circlips; a pair of snipe-nose pliers (for removing and fitting circlips); a pair of medium-size cutting pliers; a small electrical screwdriver; a six-inch steel rule; and a valve-spring compressor (*see* page 95). A gudgeon-pin extractor may also prove useful (*see* page 102), and also a magneto driving-gear extractor for sports-type models (*see* page 85). It is desirable to obtain a suitable wire brush for cleaning the sparking plug and a set of feeler gauges for checking tappet clearances, plug gap, etc., also a sparking plug re-gapping tool (*see* page 81).

For good maintenance of the motor-cycle parts you should obtain a tyre-pressure gauge (such as the Dunlop pencil type No. 6, the Romac, the Schrader No. 7750, or the Holdtite); a box of spare chain-links; a chain-rivet extractor; an extractor for the clutch centre (*see* page 113); a Lucas battery filler (*see* page 46); a hydrometer for occasionally checking the specific gravity of the battery electrolyte (*see* page 47) a chamois leather; a couple of sponges and a pail (if a hose is not available) for washing down; some soft dusters (preferably of the Selvyt type); a good wax or other polish for the enamelled parts; and a good hand-cleanser, e.g. "Swarfega."

Tools for Repair Work. Should you want to undertake as much repair work as possible in addition to general maintenance, it is obviously desirable to rig up a suitable bench, complete with vice, and to purchase some extra tools.

To begin with, it is a good plan to purchase a medium-weight hammer, a mallet, a small hand-drill and some twist-drills, a small hacksaw, a centre-punch, some large and small (smooth and rough) files, a rifler (for ports) and a good soldering outfit for repairing control cables. General repair work, however, is beyond the scope of this handbook, and you must realize that it requires appreciable technical knowledge and some genuine skill in the handling of tools. Without these assets it is best to leave well alone.

Should you wish to undertake any rebushing of the engine, this will require the use of appropriate extractors, punches, etc., a job preferably dealt with by the makers or authorized B.S.A. repairers. A selection of B.S.A. special service tools is obtainable, and details can be obtained from the makers or from any large B.S.A. spares stockist.

Keep Your A7 or A10 Model Clean. Careful and regular cleaning pays good dividends and a clean motor-cycle is always a delight to the eye.

Should you acquire a habit of allowing your machine to remain dirty, defects may pass unobserved, rusting will certainly occur, performance may decline to some extent, and depreciation of the machine will inevitably be more rapid that it should be. On no account leave your B.S.A. vertical twin soaking wet overnight. If you have not sufficient time for cleaning in wet weather, grease the machine all over *before* use.

Cleaning the Engine and Gearbox. See that the cylinder barrel and cylinder-head fins are kept clean and black (light-alloy fins excepted). If the enamel has worn off cast-iron fins, paint the fins with some proprietary cylinder-black after thorough cleaning with a stiff brush dipped in paraffin. Rusted cylinder fins besides looking shabby also reduce good dispersion of heat.

Scour off all filth from the lower part of the engine and gearbox with stiff brushes and paraffin and dry off with clean rag. Clean all aluminium-alloy and bright surfaces with a rag damped in paraffin, assisted by brushes where necessary. When stripping-down components, clean all parts with paraffin and lay on a clean sheet of paper.

Dealing with the Enamelled Parts. Never try and remove mud from the enamelled parts when dry and caked, as this is likely to damage the surfaces. If available, use a hose to soak the mud off. Where a machine is very dirty it may be advisable to paint the surfaces over with a cleaning compound such as "Gunk" before directing water on to the dirty portions. It is important to prevent any hose water and dirt getting inside vulnerable parts such as the hubs, magneto, dynamo, and carburettor. If a hose is not available, soak the mud and then disperse it with plenty of clean water, using a sponge and pail. Remove any tar spots with turpentine.

After removing all dirt, dry the enamelled parts with a chamois leather and afterwards polish them with soft dusters and some good wax polish or a proprietary polish such as "Karpol" or "Autobrite."

It is possible for "dry weather" riders to keep a motor-cycle in almost showroom condition by rubbing the enamel over with a paraffin-damped rag, followed by a dry, soft duster.

The Chromium Surfaces. Do not use liquid metal-polish or paste, as this will wear down the thin surface. It is safe, however, to use a good chromium-cleaning compound such as "Belco," but very frequent use of this is not advisable. To remove tarnish (salt deposits), clean the chromium surfaces regularly with a damp chamois-leather and then polish the surfaces with soft dusters.

To Minimize Tarnishing. It is sound policy during the winter months to wipe over occasionally all chromium-plated surfaces with a soft cloth soaked in an anti-tarnish compound such as "Tekall," obtainable in $\frac{1}{2}$ pint and 1 pint tins.

GENERAL MAINTENANCE 79

Tightness of Nuts. During the running-in period (*see* page 17) it is most advisable to apply at regular intervals some spanners to the various external nuts. Some initial bedding-down of components usually occurs Pay special attention to the engine bolts and nuts, the engine mounting-nuts, pipe unions, oil drain-plugs, etc. After a new B.S.A. vertical twin has covered about 250 miles, and also after decarbonizing, it is advisable to check tightness of cylinder-head bolts, nuts. If tightening is required, tighten the bolts in a diagonal order, and leave the *central* bolt to the last to ensure even distribution of pressure. After completing the running-in period it is sufficient to check over the various nuts for tightness about once a month. It does not take long to do this. After decarbonizing and then covering a short mileage, check over the cylinder-head and (if the barrel was removed), the cylinder-barrel nuts and/or bolts.

Adjustment and Maintenance of Carburettor. For detailed hints, see Chapter II.

Lubrication Instructions. Comprehensive instructions concerning the lubrication of 1948-62 B.S.A. vertical twins are given in Chapter III and the key on page 69 to the lubrication chart (Fig. 37) summarizes the lubrication requirements.

CARE OF THE IGNITION SYSTEM

On all 1948 and subsequent B.S.A. vertical twins the ignition system includes a very efficient Lucas magneto which has a rotating type contact-breaker and is gear-driven on the timing side by a magneto pinion. Automatic ignition-advance mechanism is in unit construction with the magneto pinion, except on sports models such as the Star Twin, Shooting Star, Road Rocket, and Super Rocket. These particular models have manual control of the ignition timing by means of a handlebar lever. An ignition cut-out button (*see* page 4) is provided on all models for earthing the primary circuit of the magneto and so stopping the engine.

Recommended Sparking Plugs. To ensure easy starting, a cool-running engine, and maximum performance throughout the throttle range, it is essential always to run on a suitable type of sparking plug. All 1948 and subsequent vertical twins require 14 mm size plugs. Four reliable and thoroughly recommended makes of sparking plugs are the Champion, the Lodge, the N.G.K., and the K.L.G. The recommended type numbers for these four makes are given in Table V. Many T.T. *winners* used N.G.K. plugs.

For regular bad-weather riding it is very advisable to fit a weatherproof terminal cover or to fit a watertight plug corresponding to the appropriate non-watertight plugs recommended in the accompanying table. Should your vertical twin have been first registered prior to 2nd, July, 1953, it is legally necessary to fit an ignition-suppression type of sparking plug, or else to fit a terminal cover with a built-in suppressor, so as not to inconvenience users of wireless and television sets. Observe that suppressor-type sparking plugs have longer wearing electrodes.

Keep the Plug Gap Correct. A recommended type of sparking plug (*see* Table V) remains serviceable for a very considerable time, but the electrode points gradually burn away and the gap between the centre electrode and the outside (earth) electrode(s) becomes excessive, causing difficult starting and occasional misfiring when riding at a reduced speed.

TABLE V. SPARKING PLUG RECOMMENDATIONS FOR B.S.A. VERTICAL TWINS

B.S.A. Model	N.G.K. Plug	Champion Plug	Lodge Plug	K.L.G. Plug
A7 Standard.	B–7HC	L–10S or L7*	H14	F80
A7 Shooting Star.	B–77 EC	NA–10 or N3*	HLN	FE80
A7 Star Twin	B–7HC	L–11S or L5*	HHN	F100
A10 Golden Flash.	B–7HC	L–10S or L7*	H14	F80
A10 Road Rocket.	B–77EC	NA–10 or N3*	HLN	FE80
A10 Super Flash.	B–77HC	L–11S or L5*	HHN	F100
A10 Super Rocket.	B–77EC	NA–10 or N3*	HLN	FE80

Note: The fairly recent new-type numbers for Champion sparking plugs are marked with an asterisk. These numbers correspond to the earlier type numbers not marked with an asterisk.

It is advisable to check the plug gap at regular intervals of 1,000–1,500 miles and to re-gap the points if necessary. Whenever you clean a plug, check the gap also. The correct gap is 0·018–0·020 in. For obvious reasons it is preferable when re-gapping to set the gap at 0·018 in.

To check the plug gap, insert an appropriate feeler gauge, or the gauge attached to a Champion re-gapping tool (*see* Fig. 41A). The gauge should *just* slide between the centre and outer electrode(s). When this occurs, note the dimension of the feeler gauge used. If an adjustment is necessary, bend the *outer* electrode(s), never the centre one, inwards slightly, using a plug re-gapping tool such as that shown in Fig. 41A. Tapping the outer electrode(s) for re-gapping is not recommended. In no circumstances attempt to tap or bend the centre electrode; this can damage the insulation and render the plug unserviceable.

Cleaning a Sparking Plug. The plug points should remain clean for a long period, provided that excessive oil is not entering the combustion chamber and that the carburettor is correctly adjusted. The bottom of the plug body should normally be smooth and black, and the centre insulation should retain its natural colour. A weak mixture causes the end of the plug to whiten, and an excessively rich mixture causes a sooty deposit. Excessive oil getting past the piston rings is indicated by a shiny black deposit and gumminess, while a heavily leaded fuel can be diagnosed by a greyish deposit.

With an engine in good condition it should not be necessary to inspect and clean the sparking plug thoroughly more often than once every 1,000–1,500 miles, but when running-in a rebored or new engine it is advisable to remove and check the plug for cleanliness at 500-mile intervals.

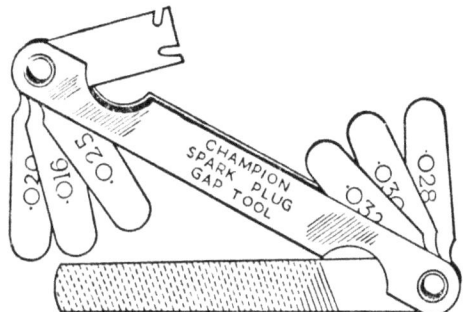

FIG. 41A. AN EXTREMELY USEFUL CHAMPION TOOL

Quick cleaning of a plug can be done by brushing the points and slightly rubbing their firing sides with some smooth emery cloth, or by using some proprietary gadget. Thorough cleaning (internal and external), however, requires that the plug be dismantled or cleaned at a garage (page 82).

Cleaning Lodge and K.L.G. Plugs. Fig. 42 shows a typical detachable type (K.L.G.) sparking plug dismantled for thorough cleaning. To dismantle a detachable-type sparking plug, grip the hexagon of the body D in a vice or with a box spanner. If you use a vice, be most careful not to exert any pressure on the hexagon faces. Then with a suitable spanner (preferably a box or ring spanner), unscrew the small hexagon B, being careful not to distort the integral metal body. The centre electrode F with its insulation (comprising the insulated electrode assembly A) can now be detached from the gland nut. Be careful not to lose the internal sealing-washer H.

To clean the "Sintox" or "Corundite" insulation, used on Lodge and K.L.G. plugs respectively, wipe it clean with a cloth soaked in petrol or paraffin. Should the insulation be coated with hard carbon deposits, remove these with some fine glass-paper, but make no attempt to scrape off the deposits. The internal sealing-washer H and the surfaces on the insulator, and in the metal body on which this washer rests, are very important as they prevent gas leakage through the plug. Therefore wipe them with a rag soaked only in petrol or paraffin. Any damage caused while dismantling will render the plug unserviceable.

To clean the metal parts (plug body and gland nut), wipe them clean with petrol, or, if necessary, scrape off the deposits with a small knife, or use a wire brush. Afterwards rinse the parts in petrol. The gland nut seldom gets very fouled, but the inside of the plug body may be very dirty, and the same may apply to the external threads of the plug. Clean and polish the points of the centre and outside (earth) electrodes F and G (Fig. 42) with some fine glass-paper.

Make sure that there is no grit or dirt lodged between the body of the plug and the insulation, and particularly on the internal-sealing washer and the contacting faces. Smear a little thin oil on the internal washer and make certain that it seats properly. When assembling the sparking plug, see that the centre electrode and insulation are positioned centrally in the body bore. If they are not, remove, re-position by rotating the centre a quarter of a turn, and re-assemble. Do not attempt to force or bend them into position.

Tighten the gland nut into the plug body only with a single-handed normal pressure applied to the tommy-bar of the box spanner or ring spanner. It is not advisable to use an open-ended spanner, as this may exert excessive pressure, resulting in distortion of the gland nut and possible damage to the insulation. Finally check that the plug gap is correct.

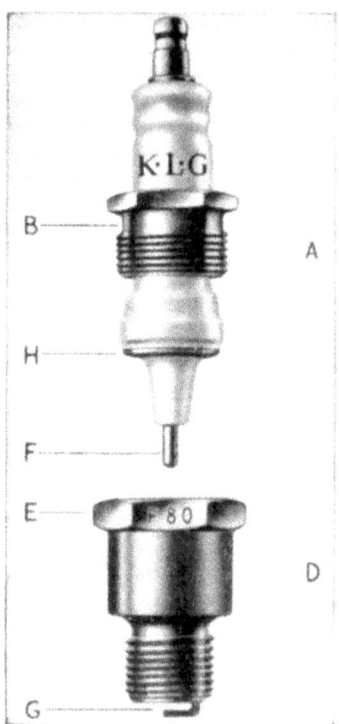

FIG. 42. DETACHABLE TYPE SPARKING PLUG (K.L.G.) DISMANTLED FOR THOROUGH CLEANING

The gland nut B and the internal sealing washer H are shown still positioned on the insulation.

Cleaning Non-detachable Plugs. A non-detachable N.G.K. or Champion plug such as the L-10S cannot be dismantled and cleaned like the detachable Lodge and K.L.G. plugs. Quick cleaning is, of course, done in the same manner (*see* page 81). The best method of cleaning any type plug thoroughly is to take it to a nearby garage having an "air-blast" unit. Within a few minutes the plug can be thoroughly cleaned of all deposits, washed, subjected to a high-pressure

GENERAL MAINTENANCE 83

air line and subsequently tested for sparking at a pressure exceeding 100 lb per sq in.

If the above method of cleaning is not available, remove the plug from the engine, pour some petrol down between the insulated centre electrode and the plug body, and set fire to the plug. Alternatively burn the plug clean with some oily rag.

To assist cleaning, use a small wire brush. Wipe the tip and outside of the insulation thoroughly clean. After removing all carbon, polish the

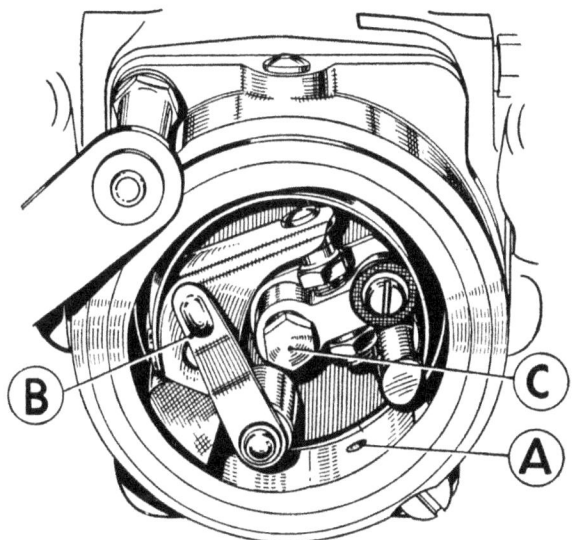

FIG. 43. MAGNETO CONTACT-BREAKER (1948–62)
    A. Oil hole.
    B. Spring clip securing rocker arm.
    C. Central bolt securing body of contact-breaker.

electrodes with some *fine* emery cloth. Finally check the plug gap (0·018–0·020 in.).

Replacing the Sparking Plug. Before replacing it, renew the steel or copper washer if worn or flattened, and clean the plug threads. Screw the plug home by hand as far as possible, and always use a box spanner for final tightening. Do not use an adjustable spanner, as this could cause some distortion.

Clean Contact-breaker About Every 5,000 Miles. The subject of lubrication is dealt with on page 66, the hole for oil insertion being shown at *A* in Fig. 43. Inspect the contacts of the contact-breaker carefully; if found to be blackened or burned, clean the contacts with some fine emery cloth or with a fine carborundum stone, removing the minimum quantity of metal necessary to thoroughly clean and true up the contacting surfaces. The correct gap is 0·010–0·012 in. with contacts fully open. Check every 3,000 miles with the gauge provided on the ignition spanner, or alternatively with a suitable proprietary feeler gauge. The gauge should be a nice sliding fit between the contacts. If the gap varies appreciably from the correct one, slacken the lock-nut on the fixed contact and turn the contact screw until the gap is found to be correct. Tighten the lock-nut.

Referring to Fig. 43, before you can detach the contact-breaker rocker arm to facilitate cleaning the contacts, you must remove the contact-breaker body from the armature body. Undo the central bolt C and firmly grip the central boss with a pair of pliers; a sharp tug should free the body from its taper. Push aside the spring clip B (or on 1961–2 models remove the spring washer) securing the rocker arm and remove the screw holding its spring to the body. You can then pull the rocker arm from its shaft. Before re-assembly make sure that everything, including the contacts, is absolutely clean.

Ignition Timing (1951–62 Models). It is most unlikely that the maker's original ignition timing will alter, provided that the contact-breaker gap (contacts fully open) is maintained at 0·010–0·012 in. A gap below and above these limits retards and advances the ignition timing respectively. Clearly if it is for any reason found necessary to check or reset the timing, it is important first to check the contact-breaker gap and adjust it if necessary as described above.

To check the ignition timing, first remove both sparking plugs, the rocker inspection covers, A, Fig. 47, and also the magneto end-cover. Next insert a thin-metal rod through the *off*-side sparking plug hole to feel the top of the right-hand piston. Turn the engine slowly (by means of the rear wheel, with top gear engaged) until the piston is at top-dead-centre (T.D.C.) on the compression stroke, i.e., with inlet and exhaust valves shut so that the rocker clearances can be felt. Keep the metal rod as vertical as possible and scratch the true T.D.C. position on it.

Now turn the engine backwards through about 45 degrees, and then bring it forward again until the contacts of the contact-breaker are just about to open. This opening position is indicated by a thin slip of cellophane or cigarette paper being lightly gripped and then withdrawn by a gentle pull.

The correct position for the piston before T.D.C. (measured by the rod through the plug hole), with the ignition fully advanced is:

A7 Standard Twin: 5/16 in.
A10 Golden Flash: 11/32 in.
All sports-type engines with high-compression pistons (7·25 to 1) : 3/8 in.
If the ignition timing does require adjustment, remove the timing cover;

GENERAL MAINTENANCE

it is secured by 12 screws of varying length, and their positions should be noted for correct replacement. With the timing cover removed, free the magneto pinion from its shaft. The central nut which locks the pinion on to the shaft, also serves as an extractor except on sports models (e.g., Star Twin, Shooting Star, Super Flash, Road Rocket, and Super Rocket). Unscrew the nut by turning it *anti-clockwise* when it will finally become tight to turn. At this point remove the "C" washer. To free the magneto pinion, deliver a sharp blow on the end of the spanner. Observe that the automatic ignition-advance mechanism, where fitted, is in unit construction with the magneto pinion, and is withdrawn with it.

On the sports models previously referred to, the magneto pinion is removed by releasing the central nut and using an extractor, Part No. 61-1903. This method is preferable to the old practice of levering the pinion off its taper with a screwdriver or other lever, because of the tendency for the *fibre* pinion to become damaged. Remove both sparking plugs and turn the engine until the timing-side piston is at the top of its stroke, using the method previously described.

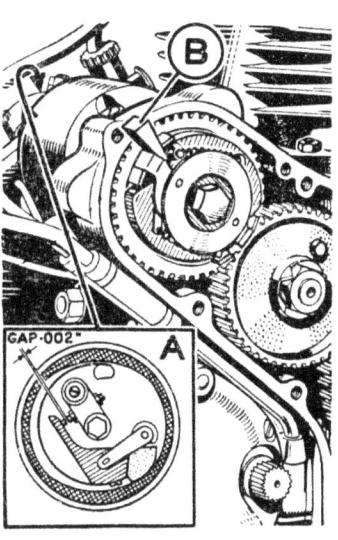

FIG. 44. AUTOMATIC IGNITION-ADVANCE UNIT WITH GOVERNOR BOB WEIGHTS WEDGED FOR TIMING CHECK

Turn the engine until the timing-side piston has descended the correct distance (5/16 in., 11/32 in., or 3/8 in.) from the top of its stroke. You can best do this turning the rear wheel by hand with top gear engaged. Some care is necessary to obtain an accurate setting. Now *fully advance* the ignition control. On the sports-type models previously mentioned, manual ignition control is provided and the ignition lever on the near side of the handlebars must be moved fully in a *clockwise* direction. On the standard Model A7 Twin and A10 Golden Flash automatic ignition-advance mechanism is provided. Set this in the following manner; turn the central bridge-plate *anti-clockwise* so that the governor bob-weights can be seen to move outwards against the resistance of the springs. This is the fully advanced position and the bob-weights should be wedged for timing purposes as shown at *B* in Fig. 44. Replace the magneto pinion loosely on its shaft so that the shaft can be moved independently of the pinion. Rotate the contact-breaker at the opposite side of the magneto in its normal direction of rotation until the contact-breaker points are just open as indicated at *A* in Fig. 44. Tap the magneto pinion home on its taper, and carefully check the ignition setting. If found correct, tighten the central nut. Do not forget to move the wedge from the governor bob-weights on models having automatic ignition-advance mechanism. Finally replace the timing cover (renew the paper gasket to ensure an oil-tight joint), the overhead-rocker inspection covers, and the sparking plugs.

To obtain a good general performance the ignition timing *must* be set correctly, and it is futile to attempt to improve on the maker's setting. This is particularly the case where automatic ignition-advance mechanism is provided, and the foregoing instructions should be most carefully observed.

The Ignition Timing (1948–50 Model A7). Do not interfere with the standard setting unless this is known to be at fault. After making a contact-breaker adjustment it is advisable, however, to check over the ignition timing, as a slight variation of the points tends to advance or retard the timing.

If the ignition timing requires to be re-set, first check that the gap between the contacts, with the contact-breaker fully open, is 0·010–0·012 in. Next remove the rocker-box caps and the sparking plug from the near-side cylinder, the timing cover, and the bolt locking the magneto pinion on its shaft. With the assistance of a magneto pinion extractor free the pinion from its taper. It should be noted that the pinion is held on its shaft by a plain taper only, and can only be freed with safety by using the proper extractor.

To set the ignition timing, turn the engine forward until the off-side piston is at the top of its compression stroke. Check its position by inserting a rod through the sparking plug hole and allowing it to rest on the crown of the piston. If with the piston at T.D.C. either of the valves is found to be partly open, this indicates that the piston is at the top of the wrong stroke, and it is therefore necessary to turn the engine through one complete revolution. If valve clearances exist for both valves, the piston is at its correct T.D.C. position for ignition timing.

After satsifying yourself that the piston is at the correct T.D.C. position, turn the engine a little further until the piston has descended exactly *one-sixteenth of an inch*. Without disturbing the position of the engine, turn the contact-breaker in its normal direction of rotation (anti-clockwise) until the contacts are just beginning to open (not more than 0·002 in.) by the action of the arm on the lower cam. Then lightly tap the magneto pinion on its taper, tighten the bolt, and carefully check the setting (i.e., piston 1/16 in. after T.D.C., points open 0·002 in.). If the setting is correct, finally tighten the magneto pinion bolt.

To obtain satisfactory engine performance the ignition timing must be correctly set. Because the engine is provided with automatic ignition-advance, it is vital that the foregoing timing instructions should be closely observed.

The Automatic Ignition-advance Unit. When occasion is had to remove the timing cover on a Standard A7 Twin or A10 Golden Flash, examine the automatic ignition-advance unit. Make sure that the governor bob-weights move freely and that if the unit is turned by hand to the advance position (bob-weights fully extended outwards) and released, the control springs withdraw the weights to the inner position (retarded). If necessary, lubricate thoroughly with engine oil.

The High-tension Pickups. About every 3,000 miles withdraw the high-tension pickups after moving the securing clips (*see* Fig. 45), wipe clean,

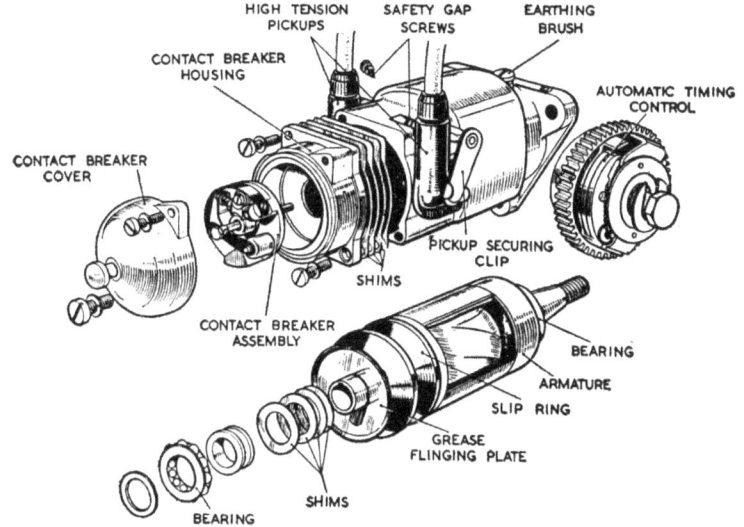

FIG. 45. EXPLODED VIEW OF LUCAS MAGNETO

and polish with a dry cloth. Each high-tension pickup brush must move freely in its holder. Should a brush be dirty, clean with a cloth moistened with petrol. Renew a brush if worn to within $\frac{1}{8}$ in. of the shoulder.

When a high-tension pickup brush is removed, thoroughly clean the track of the slip ring and its flanges by holding a soft cloth against the slip ring by means of a suitable piece of wood while slowly rotating the engine.

Renewing High-tension Cables. If on inspection either cable shows signs of perishing or cracking, replace it with a suitable length of 7-mm rubber-covered ignition cable. To fit a new high-tension cable to a pick-up terminal, bare the end of the cable for about $\frac{1}{4}$ in., thread the knurled amoulded-nut over the cable, thread the bare wire through the washer removed from the end of the old cable, and bend back the strands. Finally screw the knurled nut into the pick-up.

VALVE CLEARANCES

It is important to maintain the correct valve clearances on all B.S.A. vertical-twin engines, and the clearances should be checked about every 1,500 miles when the engine is *quite cold*; after 250 miles in the case of a new engine where considerable "bedding down" of parts occurs; and after grinding-in the valves. Note that incorrect valve clearances interfere with both the lift of the valves and also the valve timing.

Excessive clearances result in reduced valve lift and late opening of the valves which causes mechanical noise and some loss of efficiency, but this is *not* likely to damage the valves. Insufficient valve clearances, besides resulting in loss of compression, flexibility, and power, may cause distortion and perhaps burning of the exhaust valves due to gas leakage past them during the power strokes. An experienced rider can usually tell by the sound and "feel" of an engine whether the valve clearances are correct. Some appreciable variations in the cam contours of different B.S.A. vertical twins have been made and, as may be seen in Table VI, this has caused appreciable variations in the recommended valve clearances.

TABLE VI. CORRECT VALVE CLEARANCES

B.S.A. Model	Inlet	Exhaust
1948–50 A7, A10	0·015 in.	0·015 in.
1951–4 A7, A10	0·010 in.	0·010 in.
1954 A7SS	0·008 in.	0·012 in.
1954 A10RR	0·008 in.	0·008 in.
1955–9 A7	0·010 in.	0·016 in.
1955–9 A7SS	0·008 in.	0·012 in.
1955–9 A10GF	0·010 in.	0·016 in.
1955–9 A10RR, SR	0·008 in.	0·008 in.
1960–2 Models	0·008 in.	0·010 in.

Note: an inlet and exhaust valve clearance of 0·015 in. is advised for all A7 engines from No. XA7–601 to No. ZA7–11192. The first A7 engine to have 0·010 in. clearances was No. AA7102. In the first column of the above table the letters SS, RR, SR are abbreviations for Shooting Star, Road Rocket, and Super Rocket respectively.

To Make An Adjustment. Remove the sparking plugs and, referring to Figs. 46, 47, the rocker-box caps or rocker inspection covers *A* (provided on all later-type A7 and A10 engines). On the earlier 500 c.c. A7 engines with rocker-box caps remove also the four small screwed plugs *D* (Fig. 46) at the side of the rocker-boxes. Their removal facilitates easy access for checking the valve clearances with the feeler gauge provided for this purpose. On engines having rocker-box caps of the type shown in Fig. 46 the correct valve clearances are, by the way, marked on the faces of the caps.

The cams used on B.S.A. vertical-twin engines are of special design and it is therefore essential that any valve whose clearance is being checked and perhaps adjusted, should be closed, with its tappet on the base circle, or

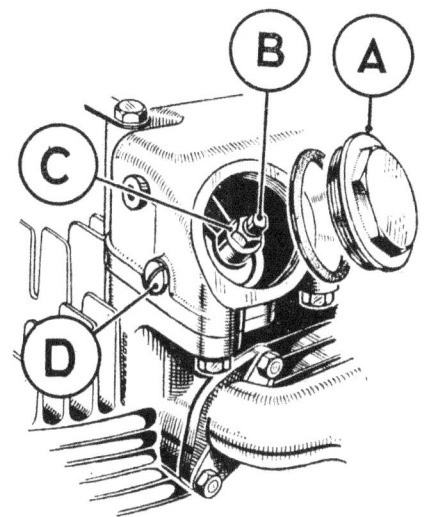

FIG. 46. VALVE CLEARANCE ADJUSTMENT
Earlier type A7 engines have rocker-box caps as shown.

neutral position of the cam. To obtain this position for the drive-side inle valve, turn the engine slowly until the *timing-side inlet valve is fully open* Similarly to set the timing-side inlet valve in the correct position, turn the engine slowly until the drive-side inlet valve is fully open. Follow the same general procedure for correctly positioning the two exhaust valves.

After turning the engine over slowly until the valve whose clearance is about to be checked, and if necessary adjusted, insert a feeler gauge of the appropriate size between the adjusting screw B (Figs. 46, 47) and the valve stem or the valve stem end cap (where fitted). If an adjustment is necessary, hold the adjusting screw B and slacken the lock-nut C. Then move the adjusting screw up or down until the valve clearance just permits the feeler gauge to enter without binding. Now, while keeping the adjusting screw absolutely stationary, firmly tighten the lock-nut C against the rocker arm. Deal with all four valves in a similar manner and when all valve clearances are found to be correct, replace the rocker-box caps or the rocker inspection covers, the screwed plugs *D* (Fig. 46), where fitted, and the two sparking plugs.

DECARBONIZING AND VALVE GRINDING

The removal of carbon deposits and the subjection of the engine to a "top overhaul" is a quite simple operation, but should only be undertaken *when the engine really needs it*. The necessity for decarbonizing is indicated

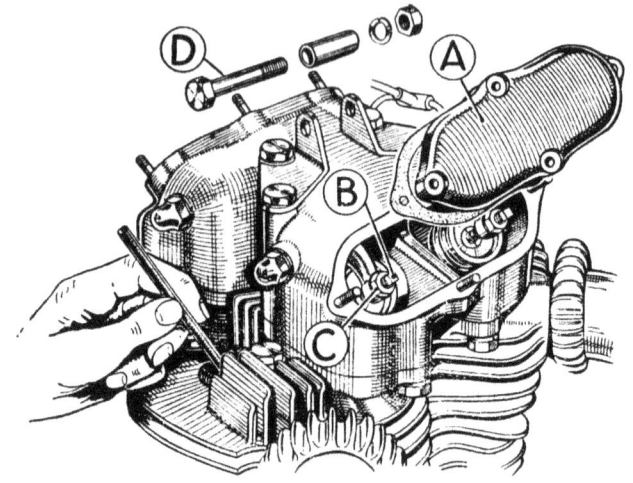

FIG. 47. VALVE CLEARANCE ADJUSTMENT

All later type A7 engines and all A10 engines have rocker inspection-covers of the type shown above. The bolt shown at *D* is for the engine-steady stay. A metal rod is shown being inserted through a plug hole to find T.D.C. for ignition timing.

by the following symptoms: (*a*) a gradual decline in the power output of the engine (especially on hills); (*b*) an increasing tendency for "pinking" (a metallic knocking sound when under heavy load); (*c*) a tendency for the engine to run hotter than normal, which is detrimental to performance and mechanical efficiency; (*d*) a tendency for the sparking plugs to become dirty rather quickly; and (*e*) some "wooliness" of the exhaust.

Valve grinding can conveniently be done when decarbonizing, and the valves and their seats should be carefully inspected.

In the normal course of events it is seldom necessary to remove the cylinder block (this requires an assistant), as "top overhaul" generally suffices to keep the machine in good running condition. Piston "slap" and bad compression, not caused by faulty valves, are symptoms which suggest the desirability of cylinder block removal so that the pistons, piston rings, and cylinder bores can be closely examined.

Petrol Tank Removal. This is essential when about to decarbonize any A7 or A10 engine. First turn off both petrol taps and remove the petrol pipes. Then proceed to remove the tank itself.

On some earlier models the speedometer is mounted on the tank; where this is the case, disconnect the speedometer drive by releasing the strainer bolt under the tank, raising the speedometer clear of the tank, and unscrewing the knurled nut connecting the drive to the instrument.

On A7 models with rigid frames or plunger-type rear springing a bolt through the steering-head lug and another bolt through the seat lug at the rear of the frame top-tube secure the petrol tank to the frame. Remove these bolts and also the saddle-nose bolt and lift the tank off.

Quickly-detachable tanks are provided on A10 models and on early machines it is only necessary to slacken the nut securing the front of the tank to the steering-head lug, and the two nuts securing the rear of the tank to the seat lug. Then lift the tank at the rear until the slotted "ears" are clear of the stud; finally pull backwards (towards the saddle) to disengage the "ears" at the front of the tank, and lift the whole assembly clear.

On all models with "swinging arm" rear suspension remove the metal strap located under the front of the tank and secured by two nuts. The central tank-locating bolt can then be removed with a box spanner (*see* Fig. 48) after the rubber plug in the top of the tank is pulled off. Then lift the tank off.

Further Preliminary Dismantling. Detach the high tension leads from the sparking plugs by means of their quick-action clips, and remove both sparking plugs. Disconnect the steady-stays from the upper part of the rocker box by unscrewing the bolt shown at D in Fig. 47. On earlier models slackening the nut at the frame end will enable the two stays to be pivoted out of the way after detaching the stays from the rocker-box.

Withdraw the Amal Standard or "Monobloc" type carburettor after removing its flange securing-bolts. If an air cleaner is fitted, slide the instrument off sideways to disconnect the rubber sleeve at its junction with the carburettor, and then tie it up out of the way. By unscrewing the ring nut at the top of the carburettor the slides can be pulled right out and also tied up when the main portion of the carburettor is removed.

The exhaust pipes are a push-in fit in the cylinder-head exhaust ports and can be pulled away, complete with silencers, when the brackets securing the exhaust system are freed by removing the securing nuts. Note that on rigid frame models the silencer brackets are attached by means of the pillion-footrest bolts.

To Remove Rocker-box and Cylinder Head (Early A7 Models up to Engine No. ZA7–11192). Remove the rocker-box connecting links and the oil feed pipe. Then remove the rocker-boxes themselves, noting that they are secured to the cylinder head by bolts above, and nuts and bolts under each box. Take off all nuts and bolts and lift the rocker-boxes clear. Remove the push-rods, noting their positions, and also (on standard A7 models) remove the hardened valve-stem end caps.

Now remove the cylinder-head retaining bolts. There are *seven* bolts. The centre bolt is inclined at an angle, and this bolt must always be removed

FIG. 48. REMOVING PETROL TANK HAVING SINGLE-BOLT FIXING

The metal strap under the front of the tank has been removed.

first and replaced last. The cylinder head unit is attached to the cylinder block at the rear by two inverted studs, and obviously it is essential to remove the nuts from these inverted studs before attempting to lift off the cylinder-head unit. The nuts are located between the fins close to the inlet manifold. Lift off the cylinder-head unit. Should it tend to stick, deliver a few sharp taps with a mallet applied below the exhaust ports.

To Remove Rocker-box and Cylinder Head (A10 and A7 Engines with Rocker Inspection Covers). Remove the oil supply pipe banjos and disconnect the oil feed pipe to the overhead rockers. Also remove the two rocker-box covers (*A*, Fig. 47). It is necessary to remove the front stud inside the rear cover before attempting to remove the rocker-box; apply the special spanner in the tool-kit to the flats machined on the stud exposed on withdrawing the cover.

Now remove the five bolts above the rocker-box, including that inside the rear tappet-cover aperture. Also remove the four nuts under the rocker-box and carefully lift the latter off. Remove all four push-rods, noting their positions to ensure proper replacement.

When the rocker-box is removed the nine bolts securing the cylinder-head unit are exposed. Remove all nine bolts (the central one first), carefully noting the positions of the different-size bolts used. They have three varying lengths. Should the cylinder-head unit stick, deliver a few light taps with a mallet applied under the exhaust ports. Carefully examine

Fig. 49. Close-up View of Typical Engine and Gearbox Assembly

the cylinder-head gasket. Scrap the existing gasket if it is not sound and bright and has black-stained patches, especially between the cylinder bores. These faults indicate gas leakage between the head and gasket, and will spoil performance.

Removing the Valves. It is normal practice to attend to the valves during decarbonizing, as this ensures a reasonable interval between valve overhaul and avoids the necessity of dismantling the engine later on. Lay a wooden block, which will fit inside the cylinder head, on a bench, and then lay the cylinder head over the block with the valve heads resting on it. Alternatively use a reliable valve-spring compressor (*see* Fig. 51), obtainable from any big accessory dealer or B.S.A. spares stockist (service tool 61–3340).

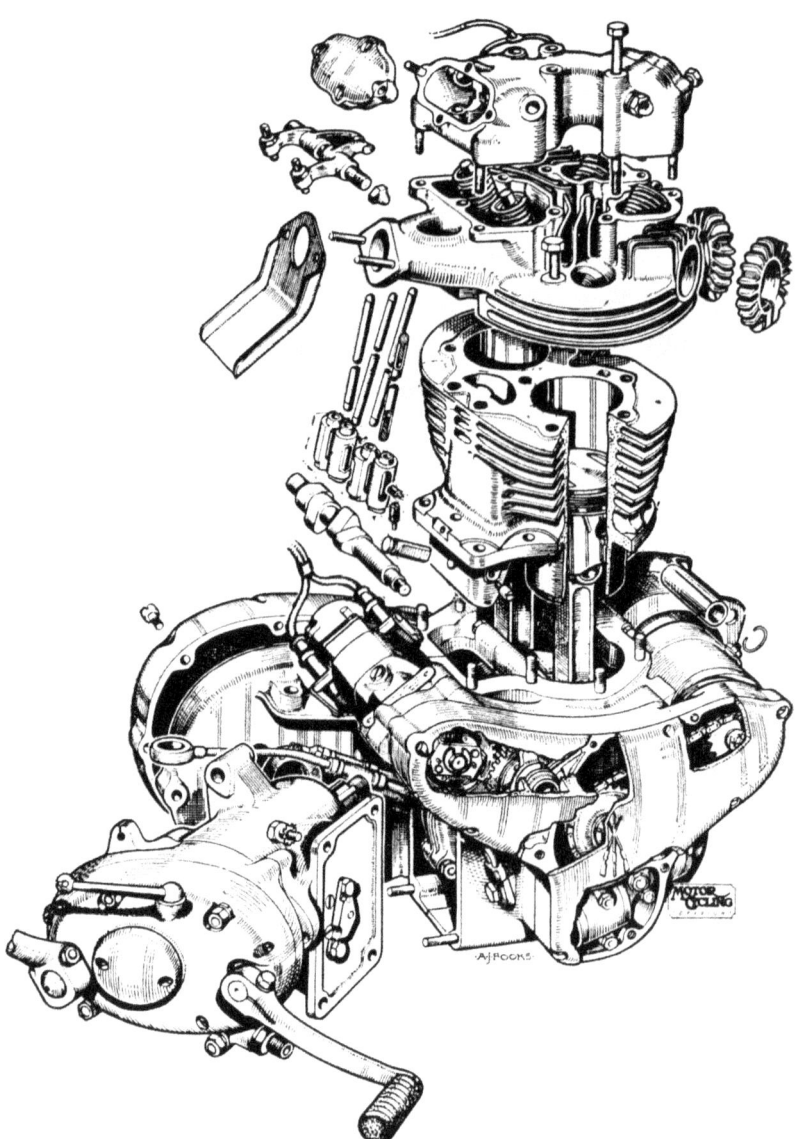

Fig. 50. Exploded View of Model A7 Power Unit
Applies to A7 engines with bolted-up gearbox (provided on plunger-sprung models) and redesigned rocker boxes.
(*By courtesy of "Motor Cycling."*)

Compress the duplex valve springs until the split collets can be removed. Afterwards lift out the valve springs, their outer collars, and valves.

Decarbonizing Pistons and Head. Thoroughness in decarbonizing well repays the labour expended. Rotate the engine by means of the kick-starter until both pistons are at the top of their strokes and proceed to chip off carefully all carbon deposits. Use a proprietary scraper, a blunt

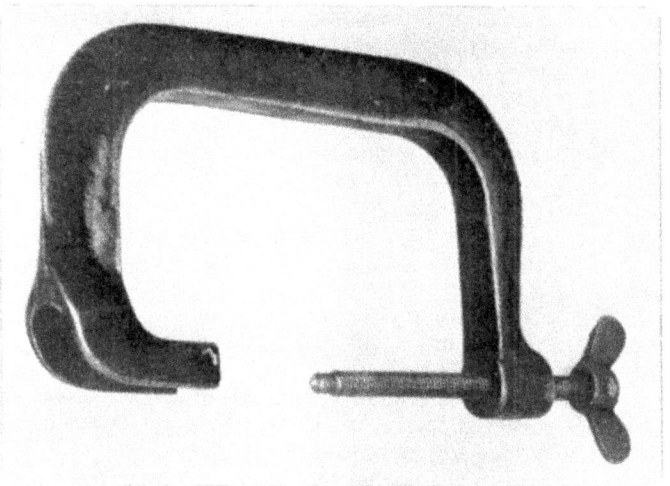

FIG. 51. VALVE-SPRING COMPRESSOR FOR A7 AND A10 ENGINES

knife, or a blunt screwdriver. Be careful not to scratch the aluminium piston-crowns, and in no circumstances attempt to polish them with an abrasive. Do not disturb slight carbon deposits on the edges.

Carefully remove all traces of carbon from the combustion chambers and ports. Take great care not to scratch the comparatively soft surface of a light-alloy head, where such is fitted. To avoid damaging the valve seats with the decarbonizing tool it is wise to insert the valves in their guides. If any carbon falls into the valve guides, remove with a piece of clean rag. The author finds that a small electrical screwdriver is an excellent tool for decarbonizing the curved walls of the combustion chambers. Do not forget to clean up both sparking-plug holes.

Examining the Valves. Examine the valve faces and also the seatings in the cylinder head. The latter deteriorate much more slowly. Any appreciable scaling or pitting indicates that the valves require to be ground-in. Very extensive pitting (usually caused by running with insufficient valve clearances, an incorrect mixture, or late ignition timing) cannot and should not be remedied by grinding-in, and it may be necessary to have the valves concerned refaced and their seatings recut by a B.S.A. repair specialist or by the Service Dept., B.S.A. Motor Cycles, Ltd., Birmingham, 11. Proper equipment is required.

Grinding-in the Valves. A special tool is provided in the tool kit for grinding-in the valves. If the valve faces and their seatings in the cylinder head are in good condition or have been refaced (45 degree angle) and recut respectively, only a very small amount of grinding-in with fine valve grinding paste is necessary to obtain a perfect gas seal. Note that an attempt to grind-in a valve having a deeply pitted face will probably induce premature wear of the seating in the cylinder head. Whatever the condition of a valve and its seating, never grind-in longer than is absolutely necessary. Excessive grinding-in can cause a valve to become "pocketed," and this inevitably reduces power output.

To grind-in a valve (see that it is the correct one), holding the cylinder head firmly on a bench, clean both the valve and its seating; smear with the finger tip or a piece of rag a thin film of fine grinding-paste (coarse at first if dealing with a valve and seat in poor condition) on the valve face; replace the correct valve in its guide minus the valve spring. Before doing this, however, it is a good plan to insert a light spring under the valve head. This greatly facilitates the grinding-in procedure and renders it unnecessary to frequently lift the valve off its seat by hand, when periodically rotating it to avoid the formation of rings or grooves.

Hold the valve with the special tool and, while maintaining a steady pressure, rotate the valve *about a third of a turn* in one direction and then an equal amount in the opposite direction, pausing every few oscillations to raise the valve from its seat to a new position. Cease grinding-in when no "cut" can be felt (and the valve begins to "sing") and put some more paste on the bevelled edge of the valve face if, after cleaning the valve with paraffin, some pitting is still visible.

Continue grinding-in until both the valve face and its seating have a uniformly smooth matt surface all round (line contact is not adequate) and there are no pit marks left after wiping the paste off. After the grinding-in of each valve is completed, wipe the valve and its seat thoroughly clean with a paraffin- or petrol-soaked rag to ensure that there is no trace of abrasive left.

The Valve Springs. While attending to decarbonizing take the opportunity of examining the duplex valve-springs. Their renewal, where necessary, is not expensive. After a considerable mileage it is generally advisable to renew the existing springs as they tend to shorten and lose their maximum efficiency under the influence of heat and continuous movement. This applies especially to exhaust-valve springs which are

GENERAL MAINTENANCE 97

subject to greater stresses than inlet-valve springs. It is bad policy and false economy to continue to use valve springs which are not in good condition, and their continued use can damage the valves besides spoiling engine performance.

When the valve springs are removed (*see* Fig. 52) compare their free lengths. Renew at once any spring which you find to be appreciably shorter

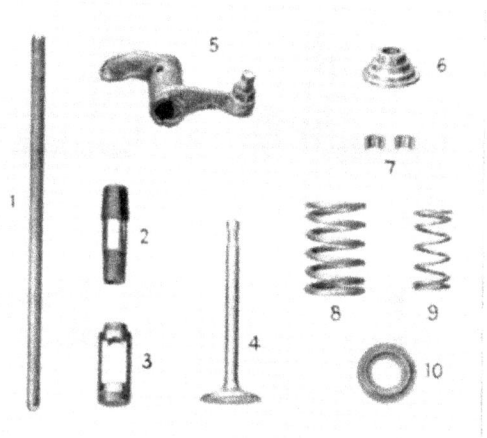

FIG. 52. SOME VALVE COMPONENTS REMOVED

Four sets of components similar to the above are of course, provided
1. Push-rod (exhaust longer than inlet).
2. Valve guide.
3. Tappet guide.
4. Valve.
5. Overhead rocker (with valve-clearance adjuster).
6. Valve-spring upper collar.
7. Split collet.
8. Outer valve spring.
9. Inner valve spring.
10. Valve-spring lower collar.

than the others, or having a free length appreciably below the standard free length for a new spring. The correct free lengths (new) are as follows: inner spring, $1\frac{17}{32}$ in.; outer spring, $1\frac{7}{8}$. 1962 SR: 2 in. and $2\frac{1}{8}$ in.

Worn Valve Guides. Valve guides wear slowly, assuming the engine is treated properly, and before deciding to renew a guide make sure that valve-stem wear is not the major cause of the valve being a loose fit in its guide. Fitting a new valve often eliminates slackness which is detected.

Where valve guide renewal is clearly called for, the worn guides must be driven out with a single suitable punch applied from inside the cylinder head. Then the new guides must be driven in from the top as far as they will go. Note that the fitting of new valve guides necessitates the valve seatings in the cylinder head being re-faced with the appropriate valve-seating cutter. This ensures that the valve seatings are absolutely concentric with the bosses of the valve guides, a most important point.

Assembling the Valves. It is assumed that all traces of grinding paste have been completely removed from the valve faces and cylinder-head

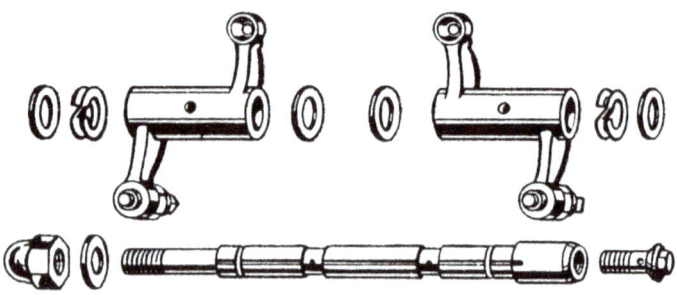

FIG. 53. ARRANGEMENT OF OVERHEAD ROCKERS AND ROCKER SPINDLE

Note carefully the disposition of the various washers. On earlier A7 engines (prior to engine No. AA7–101) a banjo oil-pipe union is fitted against the wide end of the overhead rocker spindle.

seatings. Smear each valve stem, prior to fitting the valve, with some clean engine oil. Then fit the correct valve in its guide and replace the inner and outer valve springs, and their collars, being careful not to mix up the upper and lower collars (*see* Fig. 52). Next compress the valve springs with a suitable valve-spring compressor (*see* page 93) and refit the split collet, making sure that it beds down properly on the valve-stem recess.

A blob of grease applied to the valve stem recess or the insides of the split-collet halves enables the collet to stick on the valve stem until the duplex spring is released, and it considerably facilitates assembly. Finally replace the hardened valve-stem end caps where fitted (earlier A7 type engines).

Removal of Overhead Rockers. The overhead rockers which operate the valves rarely require any attention. Should you for any reason wish to remove the rockers, do this in the following manner. Referring to Fig. 53, first unscrew the acorn nut from the end of each rocker spindle. Also disconnect the banjo oil-pipe union where fitted (*see* note below sketch, Fig. 53). Then tap out the spindle from the threaded end. To avoid damaging the threads, use a soft centre-punch applied to the threaded end exposed by the removal of the acorn nut. Note carefully the location of the seven washers, so as to ensure their correct replacement. Correct location is clearly illustrated in Fig. 53.

Removing Cylinder Block. The safe removal of the cylinder block requires the help of an assistant and is *not* necessary, or recommended, unless the condition of the engine indicates that the piston rings are in need of attention, and possibly also the pistons and cylinder bores. The usual symptoms indicating piston-ring trouble are: excessive oil consumption, excessive blue smoke issuing from the exhaust pipes, undue piston slap when the engine is warm, and reduced compression which can seriously affect engine performance.

Note that bad compression is more commonly caused by valves which need grinding-in, rather than by piston-ring trouble. The subject of examining the valves and grinding them in has already been dealt with on pages 95–6.

Piston slap besides being caused possibly by faulty piston rings, can also result from considerable wear of the cylinder-block bores. To determine this point, block removal should not be necessary. Rotate the engine until both pistons are at bottom-dead-centre. This exposes both bores sufficiently to enable a close examination to be made (*see* later paragraph), and also a dimensional check up. On new B.S.A. engines the bore is 66 mm and 70 mm for A7 and A10 engines respectively.

To withdraw the cylinder block, complete with tappets (mounted in a housing at the base of the block) rotate the engine until both pistons are at bottom-dead centre and then remove the nine cylinder-block base nuts. Now, standing astride the machine, slowly raise the cylinder block until the pistons emerge from the cylinder bores. You definitely need an assistant to steady the pistons as they clear the cylinder bores, and also for the purpose of relieving you of the quite appreciable weight of the cylinder block. Immediately the latter is removed, cover the exposed opening of the crankcase with a clean duster to prevent the accidental entry of grit, dust, and any foreign bodies. A nut, for example, falling into the crankcase can have really disastrous results!

Scrape the paper washer thoroughly from the cylinder block base flange and from the crankcase face. For cleaning up joint-faces the author advocates the use of a carpenter's scraper plate which is most helpful.

Examination of Cylinder-block Bores. Careful examination of the bores for wear should be made. Reboring may be called for if your can feel a deep ridge at the upper end of each bore, and if such is noticed you should take the cylinder block to your local dealer to decide on the matter.

Should you notice any shiny marks on a bore surface, this suggests slight piston seizure and the piston concerned should be carefully inspected and if necessary attended to. The presence of any deep scores causes loss of compression and heavy oil consumption. A rebore is the only effective remedy.

Note that pistons ½ mm and 1 mm oversize are available for rebore purposes, but in the United Kingdom you can avail yourself of the "exchange replacement system" to obtain a rebored cylinder block with pistons to match. Your local B.S.A. spares stockist will handle the matter if the cylinder block is handed over to them with appropriate instructions.

Inspecting and Handling Piston Rings. The piston rings have the important responsibility of maintaining good engine compression and their condition is therefore extremely important. Inspect them carefully. All rings must have sufficient springiness to provide a minimum free gap between the ring ends of at least $\tfrac{3}{16}$ in. when released from the cylinder bores. Renew any rings which have lost their tension and have a smaller free gap.

If all three rings on a piston have a smooth metallic outside surface, they contact the cylinder walls satisfactorily and do not normally require any attention. If, however, the surface is shiny or discoloured at some points, the rings are not making good contact with the cylinder walls, and should be renewed. All piston rings should be quite free in their grooves but have the minimum side clearance. Renew any rings which are vertically loose in their grooves, and also renew any rings having score marks.

If the piston rings happen to be stuck in their grooves, apply some paraffin, remove the rings, and clean out all carbon deposits from the grooves and the inside faces of the rings. A convenient tool for removing carbon from the ring grooves is a piece of old piston ring ground at one end like a chisel. The utmost care is required when handling piston rings. They are made of cast iron and are of very small section. The bottom scraper ring on each piston is particularly vulnerable. Note that the scraper rings used can safely be fitted either way up. When removing or fitting a piston ring, only the minimum amount of pressure outward can safely be applied, and to avoid the risk of breaking the ring it should never be opened out wider than will just enable it to slip over the crown of the piston.

To remove or fit piston rings, insert three small strips of thin sheet-metal, about ½ in. wide and 2 in. long, as shown in Fig. 54 and ease the rings off or on very gently. When removing rings note their order to ensure correct replacement. When fitting new piston rings, thoroughly clean the piston-ring grooves first because any deposit left forces out the rings and, perhaps, makes them too tight a fit. Piston rings are made to very accurate dimensions and it is most desirable always to fit rings supplied by B.S.A. Motor Cycles, Ltd. or one of their numerous dealers.

The running gap for all new piston rings should be 0·009–0·013 in.; 0·008–0·012 in. is recommended for the two top rings on 1948–50 A7 engines; although an increase of a few thousandths of an inch is not detrimental, any increase amounting to about 25 thousandths of an inch calls for ring renewal. Check the piston ring gaps occasionally with suitable feeler gauges. Place each ring in the least worn part of the cylinder

GENERAL MAINTENANCE 101

bore concerned and see that it is square in the bore by locating it with the top of the piston. If fitting a new piston ring the gap may possibly be found to be slightly less than 0·009 in. In this case clamp the ring between two wood blocks in a vice and carefully file one of the diagonal ends as required. Be careful not to enlarge the gap excessively, and see that no

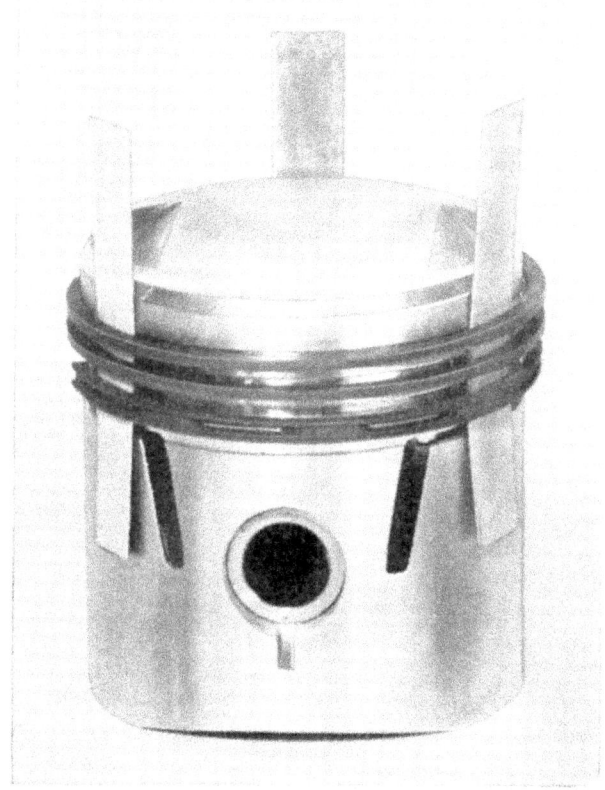

FIG. 54. SAFE METHOD OF REMOVING AND FITTING PISTON RINGS

protruding ridge is left on the end of the ring; this could score the cylinder bore.

If a new piston ring is found to be a tight fit in its groove, rub down one side of the ring on a piece of carborundum paper laid on a sheet of glass.

Piston Removal. It is quite unnecessary to remove the pistons unless heir condition is such that they require to be renewed, or unless for some reason major dismantling of the engine becomes necessary. If you decide to remove the pistons, remove each one as described below.

Insert a pointed instrument such as the suitably ground tang-end of a small file in the appropriate piston notch and prise out one of the wire circlips which retain the fully-floating gudgeon-pin in position. This circlip should be discarded after removal, as it is the safest policy always

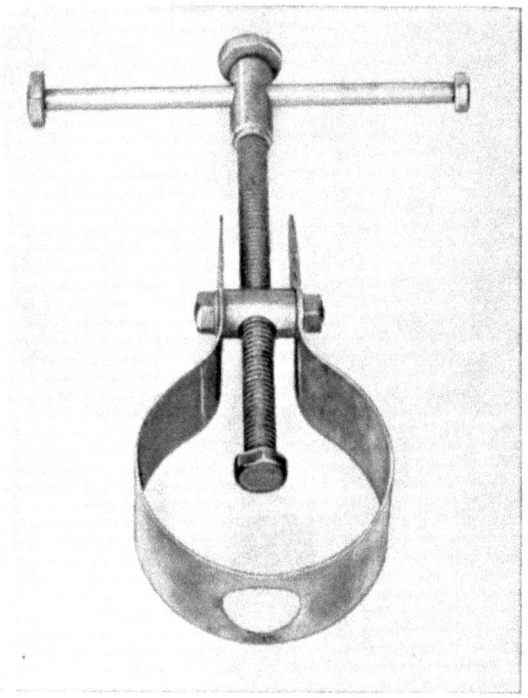

FIG. 55. PROPRIETARY TOOL FOR PRESSING GUDGEON-PIN IN OR OUT

Note the three different size pressure-pads on the ends of the tommy-bar and the pressure screw. They, of course fit different size gudgeon-pins.

to fit a new B.S.A. circlip when replacing a piston. A circlip which accidentally comes adrift can have disastrous results.

When the engine is cold the gudgeon-pin is a tight fit in the piston bosses and prior to removing it *first warm the piston* by wrapping it with a cloth previously immersed in boiling water and wrung out, or else by laying an electric iron on the crown of the piston.

When the piston is thoroughly warm press out the gudgeon-pin, using a proprietary tool such as that shown in Fig. 55. Alternatively tap out the

GENERAL MAINTENANCE

pin with a suitable-diameter punch and a light hammer. If the latter method is used, it is essential to support the piston on the side opposite to that where the hammer is being applied. Failure to provide support can cause an excessive side stress to be imposed on the connecting-rod.

On removing the gudgeon-pin make a slight nick on one end to ensure the pin being subsequently fitted the correct way round. Super Rocket engines do not have split-skirt type pistons and with such engines it is desirable to scratch an "F" on the inside of each piston to indicate which is the front. Always remember that a light-alloy piston must be handled with great care; it can be very easily cracked or distorted.

Replacing Pistons. Be quite sure to replace each piston on the connecting-rod from which it was removed. Except on Super Rocket engines both pistons have split skirts and *the diagonal cut must face to the front.* Warm each piston before inserting the gudgeon-pin which should be smeared with oil. Press or tap the pin home, using the same procedure as that employed for removal. Fit the new wire circlip and make absolutely certain that it beds down snugly and is secure. This is most important.

Replacement of Cylinder Block. Fit a new paper washer to the crankcase face after lightly smearing it with some good jointing compound. Liberally rub some clean engine oil over both pistons and also the cylinder bores. Space the piston rings so that their gaps are at 120 degrees to each other and position the pistons so that they are at bottom-dead-centre. Then with assistance proceed to fit the cylinder block over the pistons.

Before actually fitting the cylinder block it is advisable to compress the piston rings in their grooves, by means of B.S.A. piston-ring compressors. These are available as extras for A7 and A10 type engines. Also make up two strips of wood of $\frac{3}{4}$ in. square section and about 8 in. long. Lay both strips of wood across the crankcase mouth beneath the pistons, one at the front and the other at the rear. The purpose of doing this is to hold the two pistons quite square and steady during the lowering of the cylinder block. The pistons are shown ready to receive the cylinder block in Fig. 56.

Carefully and slowly lower the cylinder block over the two pistons. Immediately the pistons enter the cylinder bores the piston-ring compressors will automatically be slid off the pistons and, together with the two wooden piston-steadies, can be withdrawn before the cylinder block is finally lowered on to the crankcase-face washer.

To Replace Cylinder Head and Rocker-boxes (A7 Models up to Engine No. ZA7–11192). Lay the four push-rods in their respective tappets (the exhaust push-rods are longer than the inlet ones) and then position the gasket and cylinder head. Fit the *seven* cylinder-head securing bolts and also the nuts on the two inverted studs (located between the fins near the inlet manifold) at the rear. Tighten evenly and firmly, and in a diagonal order, the seven bolts and two nuts. *The centre bolt, inclined at an angle, should be fitted and tightened last.*

Check that the valve stem end-caps (where fitted) are replaced. Next replace the two rocker-boxes and see that the four push-rods are properly

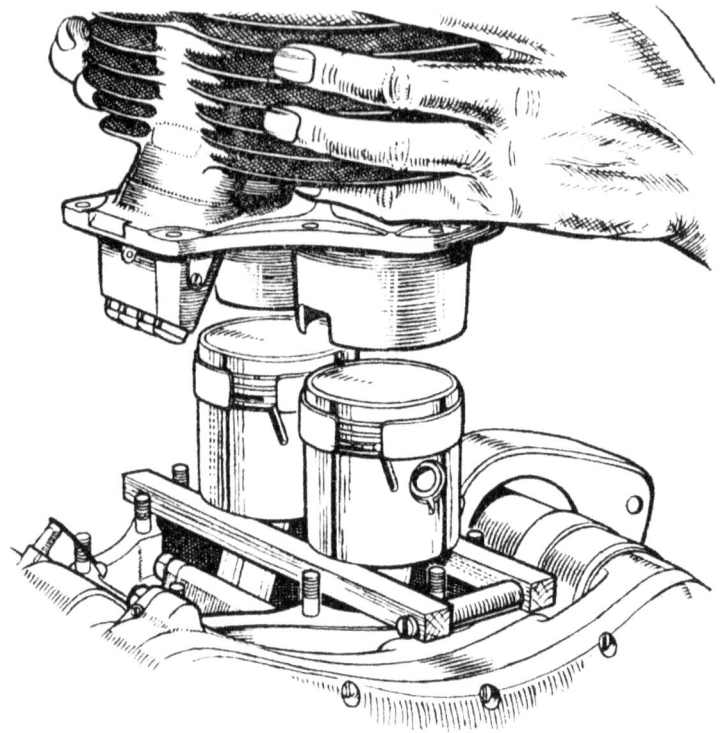

FIG. 56. REPLACING THE CYLINDER BLOCK

This satisfactory method is used by the B.S.A. factory. Note the two strips of wood for steadying the pistons and the B.S.A. piston-ring compressors.

(*By courtesy of "Motor Cycle," London.*)

located in the rocker ends. Tighten securely and evenly the bolts above and the nuts below each rocker-box. Before replacing the rocker-box caps, check the valve clearances (*see* page 88) and if necessary make the required adjustment. Replace the rocker-box connecting links and the engine steady-stay, also the oil-feed pipe.

To Replace Cylinder Head and Rocker-box (A10 and A7 Engines with Rocker Inspection Covers). Replace the cylinder head gasket and position the cylinder head. Fit the nine bolts securing the cylinder head in their

GENERAL MAINTENANCE

correct positions (there are three different sizes), and to avoid the risk of distorting the head tighten down the nine bolts evenly and firmly in the sequence shown in Fig. 57.

Replace the four push-rods, inserting them through the apertures provided in the cylinder head. See that their lower ends fit properly into their respective tappet cups and note that the two inlet push-rods are

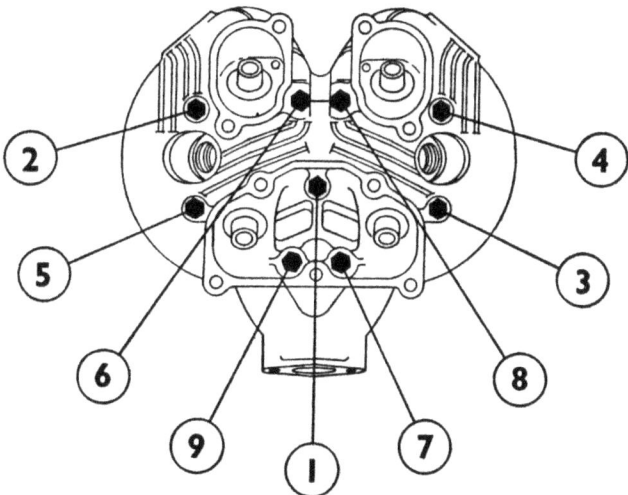

FIG. 57. THE CORRECT SEQUENCE FOR TIGHTENING THE CYLINDER HEAD BOLTS

shorter than the exhaust rods. Fit the rocker-box and make sure that the upper ends of the push-rods enter the recesses in the ends of the inner overhead-rocker arms.

Replace the five bolts above the rocker-box, including that inside the rear tappet cover aperture, and also the four nuts below the rocker-box. Tighten down all bolts and nuts evenly and in a diagonal order, and do not forget to replace the engine steady-stays (secured by bolt *D*, Fig. 47) as soon as the rocker-box is finally bolted down.

Before replacing the rocker-box covers (*A*, Fig. 47) check the valve clearances (*see* page 88) and where necessary adjust them. Reconnect the oil-feed pipe to the rocker spindles.

Final Assembly. Replace the standard or "monobloc" type Amal carburettor. If an air cleaner is fitted, attach the rubber connexion to the carburettor *before* it is finally bolted to the cylinder head. Clean the sparking plugs and if necessary adjust their gaps (*see* pages 80–3) and reconnect the high-tension leads, being sure that each high-tension lead is connected to the correct sparking plug. Replace both push-in fit exhaust pipes, complete with silencers, and secure the brackets holding them to the frame. On rigid-frame models firmly tighten the pillion-footrest bolts which secure the silencer brackets.

Replace the petrol tank and the petrol pipes. On earlier models with a tank-mounted speedometer connect up the speedometer drive and light

Fig. 58. Close-up View of Completely Assembled Engine

cable. Securely tighten the strainer bolt under the petrol tank. Also firmly tighten the tank-securing bolts or nuts at the front and rear. On "swinging arm" models tighten with a box spanner the central tank-locating bolt after replacing the metal strap under the front of the tank. Afterwards replace the rubber plug over the central locating-bolt. Reassembly of the engine is now complete and you can start her up. After a comparatively short mileage (about 250 miles) on the road it is advisable to check over the various external nuts and bolts on the engine for tightness and tighten further if required.

VALVE TIMING

Do not dismantle the timing gear unless this is absolutely necessary. Under normal running conditions it is quite impossible for the valve timing to be disturbed. The correct valve timings for all 1948–62 A7 and A10 engines be shown in Fig. 59. Should a check of the valve timing for some reason reconsidered necessary, observe the following procedure and sequence.

Preliminary Dismantling. First remove the timing cover securing-screws. These screws vary in length and their correct positions should therefore be noted. Remove the dynamo chain and the large sprocket which must both be taken off together, the chain being of the endless type with no connecting link.

To avoid possible damage to the timing cover it is advisable after removing the nut and locking washer to use an extractor to remove the large sprocket which fits on a tapered shaft and has no key. An alternative

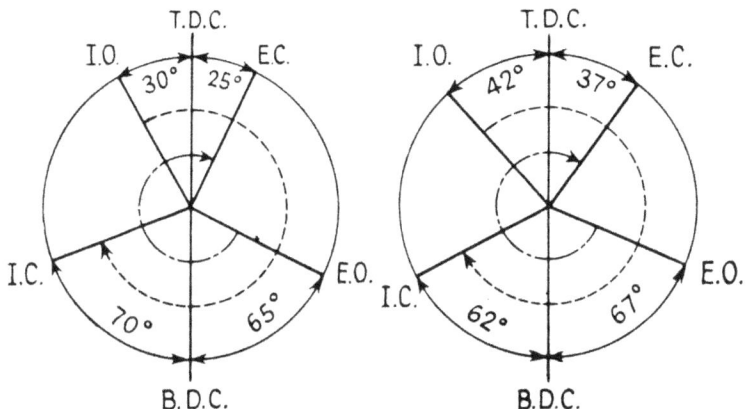

FIG. 59. VALVE TIMING DIAGRAMS FOR 1948–62 A7 AND A10 ENGINES

On the left is the maker's valve timing for standard-type A7 models and the A10 Golden Flash. On the right is the valve timing employed for 1951–8 sports-type A10 models, e.g., the Star Twin, Road Rocket, Super Rocket, and Shooting Star. This valve timing also applies to all 1959–62 engines (standard and sports).

is to apply a spanner to the dynamo-sprocket nut and deliver on it a sharp tap clockwise, with the dynamo chain in position. The large sprocket should then be freed and when removed from its spindle the dynamo chain can be removed from the small sprocket which remains in position on the spindle of the dynamo.

Slacken the dynamo strap so that the dynamo can be rotated by hand to a suitable position to enable its sprocket to pass through the aperture in the timing cover when this is removed. Withdraw the cover which is held by four screws. It may be found that the breather sleeve will remain in the timing cover, leaving the cork washer sticking to the camshaft gear.

To Check the Timing. Examine the camshaft gears and satisfy yourself that the timing markings are positioned exactly as indicated in Fig. 60. Rotation of the engine several times may be required to enable the timing markings to line up as illustrated.

During Reassembly. See that the breather cork-washer is perfect. If it is not, renew it. See that the driving peg in the camshaft gear engages with the hole in the breather sleeve. After tightening the nut securing the large dynamo chain-sprocket do not forget to bend the locking washer into position. Prior to tightening the strap securing the dynamo, firmly push the dynamo against the back of the timing case. This traps the oil seal and ensures an oil-tight joint. Renew the paper washers between the cover joint-faces.

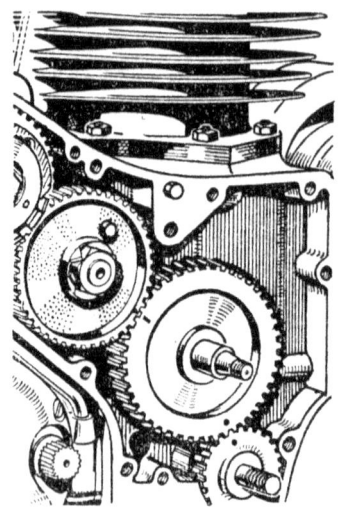

FIG. 60. TIMING GEAR MARKS ALIGNED TO GIVE CORRECT TIMING

The dot and dash system shown is used on all A7 and A10 engines.

CARE OF THE TRANSMISSION

Clutch Control Adjustment. It is important always to maintain about $\frac{1}{8}$ in. free movement of the clutch control cable at the handlebar end. Absence of any backlash generally causes clutch slip and subjects the friction inserts to unnecessary wear. Excessive backlash gives rise to clutch drag and general inefficiency of clutch operation. Note that normal wear of the friction inserts gradually decreases the backlash.

Referring to Fig. 61, if a clutch adjustment is required remove the two screws and withdraw the oval-shaped inspection cover from the off side of the gearbox. Be careful not to damage the gasket. Then loosen the lock-nut (G) and turn the small adjuster screw (H) so that when the clutch is fully withdrawn the long operating-lever on top of the gearbox is at right-angles to the clutch push-rod. This ensures the minimum side thrust being imposed on the push-rod. Afterwards tighten the lock-nut G securely and carefully turn the knurled hand-adjuster at (E) until the required $\frac{1}{8}$ in. backlash in the cable is obtained.

Primary Chain Adjustment ("Swinging Arm" Models). Occasionally (about every 2,000 miles) remove the oil-bath chain case inspection cap shown at (C) in Figs. 38 and 40. See that the total up-and-down movement of the primary chain near its centre, with the chain in its tightest position, does not exceed $\frac{1}{2}$ in. If the chain-case cover happens to be removed, check the chain whip in the centre of the bottom chain run.

Referring to Fig. 61, to pivot the gearbox backwards in order to take up excessive chain slackness, loosen the large lock-nuts (A) and (B). Note that the lock-nut (B) also secures the adjuster in position. Then loosen the lock-nut (C) on the adjuster, and to tighten the primary chain turn the adjuster (D) *clockwise* as required to pivot the gearbox backwards the required amount. Finally tighten the lock-nut (C) and nuts (A) and (B). Afterwards check the tension of the secondary chain as described in a later paragraph. Its tension is sure to have altered.

Primary Chain Adjustment (Models with Plunger Type Rear Springing). On many A10 Golden Flash models with plunger type rear springing a

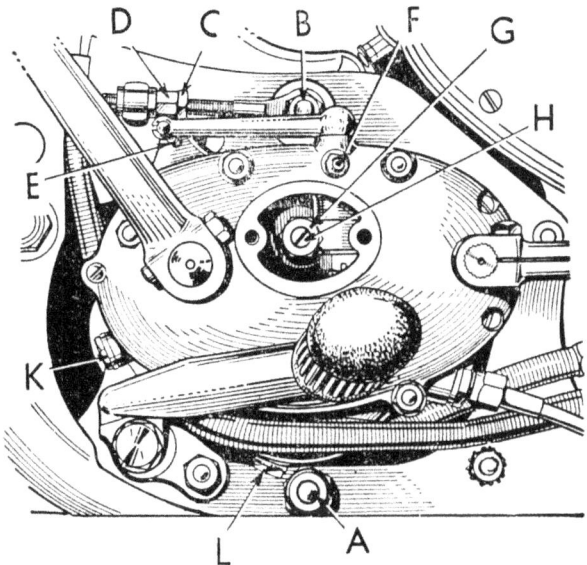

FIG. 61. CLUTCH AND PRIMARY CHAIN ADJUSTMENT ("SWINGING ARM" MODELS)

duplex primary chain is fitted and this has a special tensioner (*see* Fig. 62). To check the chain tension remove the oil-bath filler cap and feel the total up and down movement which should be approximately $\frac{1}{2}$ in.

To reduce the chain tension, slacken lock-nut (B), screw the adjuster (C) downwards, and apply pressure on the kick-starter pedal. By this means the tensioning "slipper" will move down and slacken the chain. To tighten the chain, screw the adjuster (C) upwards.

Increasing Clutch Spring Pressure (All Models). After your A7 or A10 model B.S.A. has covered a considerable mileage wear of the clutch inserts may necessitate an adjustment being made of the clutch spring pressure. Adjust as described below.

To expose the clutch assembly remove the near-side footrest and the primary chain-case cover. When doing this note the positions of the various screws to ensure their being correctly replaced. On the "swinging arm" models there are (*see* Fig. 38) three (larger diameter) short screws at the front end, six long screws at the rear, and six intermediate size screws in between; there are also, except on models having plunger-type rear springing and on 1960-2 models, two red painted screws (*A*) and (*B*). On 1948-55 models having plunger-type rear springing there is only *one* red screw,

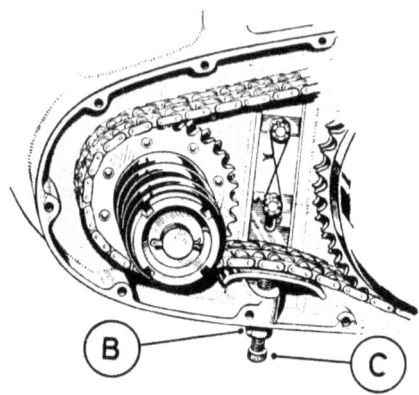

Fig. 62. Primary Chain Adjustment (Models with Plunger Type Rear Springing)

and there is a circular clutch cover secured to the clutch sprocket member by twelve screws and spring washers.

Six springs (four, 1960-2 models) are provided to keep the clutch plates pressed together and the pressure of the springs is controlled by the adjuster nuts shown at (*B*) in Fig. 63. Lock-nuts (*A*) are provided on most "swinging arm" models but are omitted in 1948-55 models having plunger-type rear springing (*see* Fig. 65) and on 1960-2 models. Where lock-nuts are fitted, loosen with a box spanner each lock-nut while holding the adjuster nut (*B*) stationary with another spanner.

To maintain true alignment of the clutch plates, and to avoid clutch drag, it is essential to tighten all six adjuster nuts (*B*) *the same number of turns*. Withdraw the clutch to ensure that it frees freely and check that the end plate does not tilt. If any tilting occurs, adjust the nuts (*B*) as required.

Where lock-nuts are provided ("swinging arm" models) tighten these firmly and then replace the clutch cover (where fitted), the oil-bath chain case cover, and the near-side footrest. Be sure to fit the red-painted screws (where provided) correctly. Finally test the clutch by disengaging it and spinning the driving plates by means of the kick-starter.

GENERAL MAINTENANCE

Dismantling the Clutch (1948–59). Expose the B.S.A. clutch assembly (*see* page 110) and on 1948–55 models with plunger-type rear springing withdraw the cover shown in Fig. 65 after removing the twelve screws and spring washers.

The six clutch spring adjuster-nuts and (on "swinging arm" models) lock-nuts, and also the spring plate should now be removed. Unscrew the

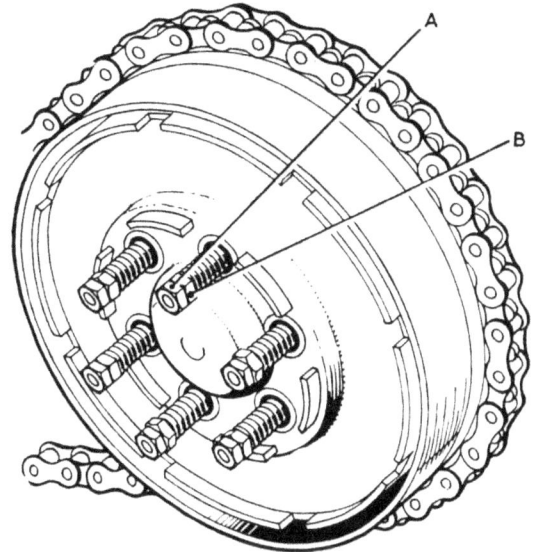

FIG. 63. ADJUSTMENT OF CLUTCH SPRING TENSION (1955–9 "SWINGING ARM" MODELS)

mainshaft nut after bending back the locking washer. To prevent the mainshaft turning, engage top gear and apply the rear brake. Having removed the mainshaft nut, withdraw the complete clutch assembly, with the exception of the central splined sleeve, from the splines on the gearbox mainshaft.

Wash the clutch plates in petrol so as to remove all surplus oil, and carefully examine the plates. Glazed friction plates and scored plain steel plates should be renewed. Badly worn inserts should be replaced.

Examine the clutch sprocket member and the clutch body for burrs which can prevent the plates sliding freely. Remove any slight burrs with a smooth file. If your mount has done a very considerable mileage, examine the clutch sprocket teeth for wear, remembering that worn teeth greatly accelerate wear of the primary chain. Note that the ball race should

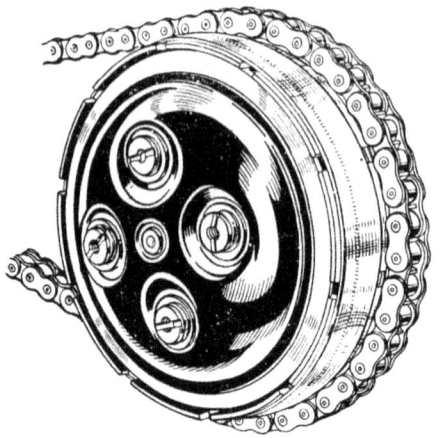

Fig. 64. Clutch Spring Adjustment (1960–2 "Swinging Arm" Models)

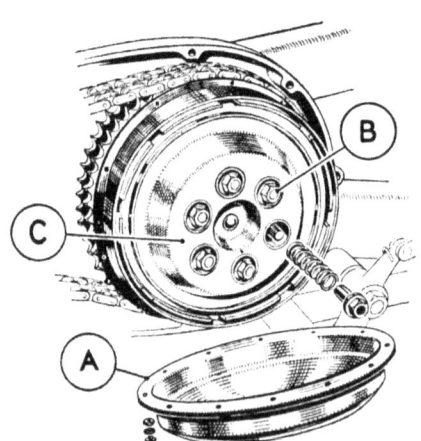

Fig. 65. Clutch Spring Adjustment (1948–55 Models with Plunger Type Rear Springing)

    A. Domed clutch cover
    B. Spring-tension adjuster nuts
    C. Clutch outer plate

not have more than 0·0015 in. diametral play, otherwise there may be a tendency for clutch slip to occur.

After replacing the clutch assembly in the reverse order of dismantling, see that the mainshaft nut is securely tightened after correctly locating its locking washer on the splined sleeve. Turn down the washer over the flat on the outside of the mainshaft nut.

The Splined Sleeve (1945-59). The sleeve fits on the tapered end of the gearbox mainshaft and is located by a detachable key. To remove the splined sleeve it is necessary to employ a special screwed extractor (Part No. 61-3362), obtainable from a B.S.A. spares stockist.

Dismantling the Clutch (1960-2). Remove the four slotted spring retaining-nuts and withdraw the clutch pressure plate. Then remove the

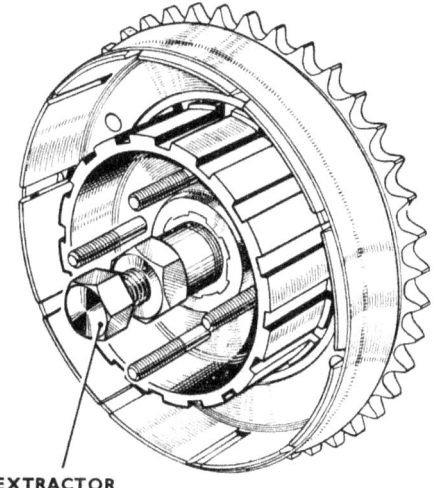

EXTRACTOR

FIG 66. SHOWING B.S.A. EXTRACTOR REQUIRED FOR REMOVING CLUTCH BODY AND SPLINED SLEEVE

clutch plates. If inspection of the driven plates shows that the bonded segments are damaged, renew. Also renew any scored driving (plain) plates.

Should removal of the body of the clutch be necessary, use the B.S.A. extractor (Part No. 69-1912). First bend back the tab of the locking washer and then remove the central nut. Engage fourth gear and apply the rear brake in the event of difficulty being encountered due to shaft rotation. At this stage avoid pulling the clutch outwards, otherwise the rollers from the clutch bearing may fall out and be mislaid. Now apply the extractor (*see* Fig. 66) and remove the clutch body together with the splined sleeve. By laying the clutch horizontally on a bench the clutch body can be lifted off the splined sleeve without disturbing the rollers.

Examine the slots on the chain wheel, and the central cage, for irregularities and burrs which may prevent the plates sliding freely. Slight irregularities can be removed with a smooth file. Where the motor-cycle has covered a considerable mileage, examine the sprocket teeth for wear likely to cause deterioration of the secondary chain.

When assembling the clutch, proceed in the reverse order of dismantling. Grease the rollers to facilitate replacing the chain wheel and splined sleeve. After correctly locating the locking washer make sure that the large central nut is firmly re-tightened. Finally prize up the tongues on the locking washer and impress them against the flat of the nut.

Primary Chain Case Removal ("Swinging Arm" Models). The outer cover can be withdrawn after removing the left-hand footrest and the 15 cover-retaining screws. To permit further dismantling, you must remove the engine sprocket and clutch. The rear of the oil-bath chain case is secured to the crankcase by three bolts behind the engine sprocket, and these can be undone after breaking the locking wire through the head of the bolts. A single bolt at its lower rear end secures the rear of the chain case to the frame.

Secondary Chain Adjustment (Models with Plunger Type Rear Springing). Check the tension of the secondary chain about every 1,000 miles and make an adjustment if it is found that the chain has stretched. If you have just adjusted the tension of the primary chain, an adjustment of the secondary chain tension is almost sure to be needed.

To check the chain tension, place the motor-cycle on its central stand so that the rear wheel is in its lowest position. Observe whether the total up-and-down movement obtainable at the centre of the bottom run, with the chain in its tightest position, is correct, namely about $\frac{1}{2}$ in.

Referring to Fig. 67, to re-tension the secondary chain, with the machine on its central stand, slacken the knurled hand adjuster for the rear brake. Then with the appropriate spanner loosen nut (A), and with a tommy bar applied at (C), loosen the rear wheel spinndle. Now slacken the hexagon (B) on the near-side spindle end and, with a suitable spanner, screw the adjustors (D) *evenly* in or out as required to effect the correct chain tension. Finally tighten firmly nuts (A) and (B) and re-adjust the rear brake and check that the wheels are in true alignment (*see* page 123).

Secondary Chain Adjustment (Models with "Swinging Arm" Rear Suspension). About every 1,000 miles check the tension of the secondary chain when in its tightest position and with the machine resting on its central stand. On 1956-62 models having a pressed-steel chain case removal of the front rubber plug (*see* Fig. 70) gives access to the chain for checking its tension. The total up-and-down movement (whip) at or near the centre should be $1\frac{1}{4}$ in. This movement is, of course, substantially decreased when the rider is seated with the machine off its stand.

Referring to Fig. 68, an adjustment for chain tension when required should be effected in the following manner. Slacken off the brake adjuster,

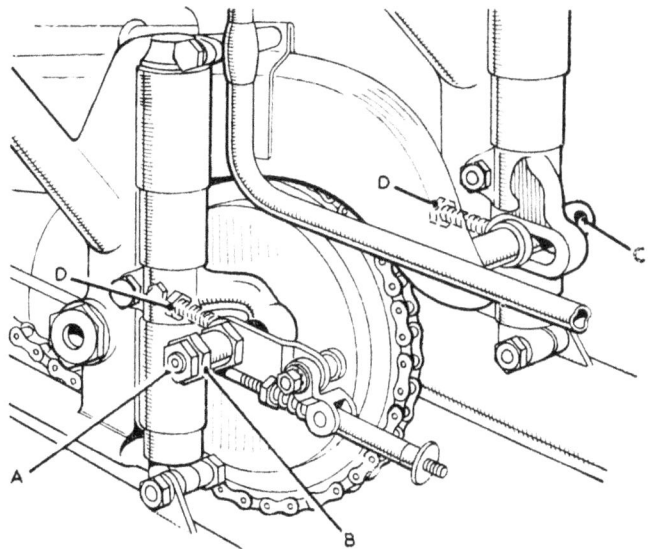

FIG. 67. SECONDARY CHAIN ADJUSTMENT ON 1948-55 MODELS HAVING PLUNGER TYPE REAR SPRINGING

unscrew the spindle (*B*) and then slacken the hexagon on the near side of the wheel hub. Loosen the lock-nuts (*D*) and screw the adjusters (*E*) *evenly* in or out as required until the correct chain tension is obtained. If the secondary chain is not totally enclosed, it is best to check the tension at the centre of the bottom run. Re-adjust the rear brake and, if you have the slightest doubt about the wheel being truly aligned, check wheel alignment (*see* page 123).

Secondary Chain Adjustment (Rigid Frame Models). Check the tension of the secondary chain about every 1,000 miles. If the total up-and-down movement obtainable in the centre of the lower chain run, with the chain in its tightest position, is excessive, re-tension the chain. The correct total movement is $\frac{3}{4}$ in.

To re-tension the secondary chain, place the machine on its stand and slacken off the knurled hand adjuster on the rear brake rod. Then, referring to Fig. 69, loosen the spindle nut (A) sufficiently to allow of the wheel spindle being moved. Now insert a suitable tommy bar into the

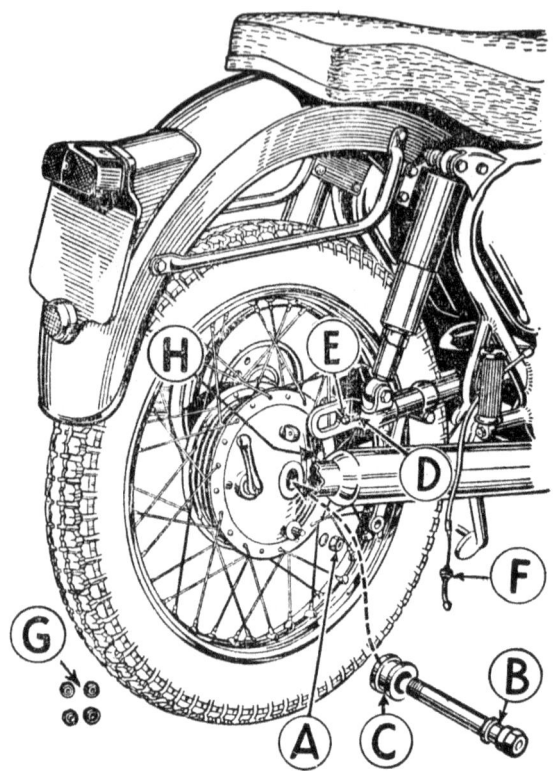

Fig. 68. Secondary Chain Adjustment and Removal of Quickly-detachable Rear Wheel (Full Width Hub) on 1956–62 "Swinging Arm" Models

spindle head (B) and unscrew the spindle (right-hand thread) a short distance. Slacken the two lock-nuts (D) and then screw inwards the adjusting pins (C) against the wheel spindle until it has moved backwards enough to enable the correct chain tension to be obtained. Be careful to turn the adjusting pins (C) an equal amount, otherwise the alignment of the wheels will be disturbed. Finally re-tighten the lock-nuts (D), the spindle (B), and the spindle nut (A). Also carefully adjust the rear brake.

GENERAL MAINTENANCE 117

Stretch of Chains. It is advisable to renew immediately any primary or secondary chain when the degree of stretch present exceeds *a quarter of an inch per foot*. To test a chain for stretch, close up about one foot of the chain's length, measure the exact length, pull the links apart, and again measure the length. The difference between the two measured lengths is the amount the chain has stretched.

The Gearbox. The author does not advise the average B.S.A. owner to dismantle the gearbox and attempt major repairs himself. The work

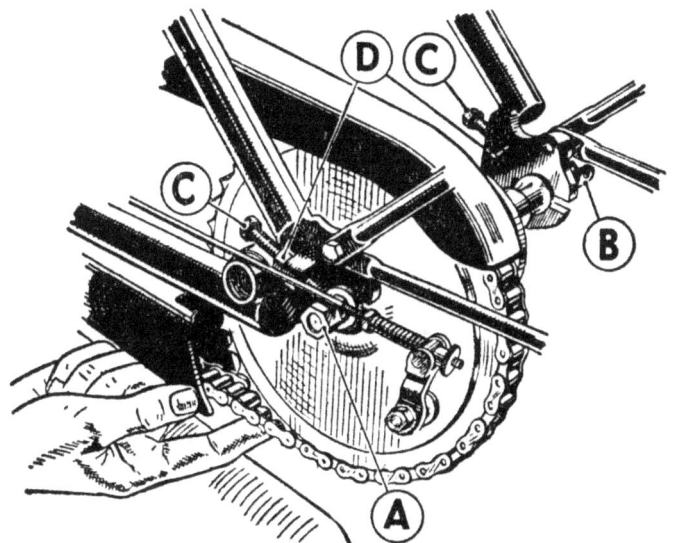

FIG. 69. SECONDARY CHAIN ADJUSTMENT (RIGID FRAME MODELS)

requires a considerable amount of skill and experience and is best entrusted to B.S.A. Motor Cycles, Ltd. or an approved B.S.A. repair specialist. Fortunately gearbox trouble is rare, and in the unlikely event of your needing to remove the complete gearbox assembly from the frame, or engine and frame (1948–55 models), observe closely the appropriate instructions given in the maker's instruction manual.

To Remove Rear Wheel ("Swinging Arm" Models). The rear wheel is of the quickly-detachable type and has ball journal-type non-adjustable bearings. Referring to Fig. 68, to remove the rear wheel, first jack the machine up on its central stand. On all models with full-width light-alloy rear hub, remove the nut (*A*) so as to free the brake anchor-strap. Also disconnect, as shown, the rear-brake operating cable (*F*). Remove the four nuts (*G*) which secure the light-alloy hub to the boss of the chain sprocket. These nuts are accessible on the near side and, on machines provided with a chain case, can be removed individually with a box spanner after first withdrawing the rubber plug (the rear one) as shown in Fig. 70.

Now on all models apply a spanner (tommy bar on some earlier models) to the end of the rear wheel spindle (*B*), and unscrew it *anti-clockwise* until

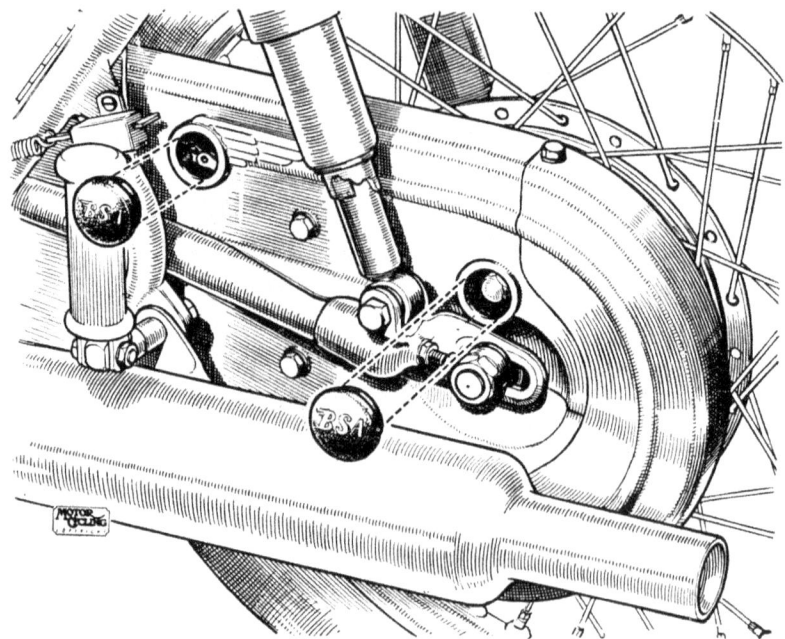

FIG. 70. COMPLETE SECONDARY CHAIN ENCLOSURE

The chain case illustrated is an optional extra. Note the two rubber plugs for holes giving access to the secondary chain and the four nuts securing the quickly-detachable wheel to the chain-sprocket boss.

(*By courtesy of "Motor Cycling"*)

it can be pulled clear. Remove the distance-piece (*C*), ease the hub to the offside until it clears the sprocket boss (brake drum on earlier models), and withdraw the wheel downwards and to the rear. Do not disturb the large nut on the near-side of the spindle.

Note that when removing the rear wheel on all models, do not disturb the large nut (*see* Fig. 70) on the near-side; this nut secures the sprocket boss or brake drum (earlier models). Also note that when replacing the

GENERAL MAINTENANCE

rear wheel on models with a full-width light-alloy hub it is very important to tighten securely the four nuts (G, Fig. 68) which secure the light-alloy hub to the sprocket boss.

The Bearings (Full-width Light-alloy Hubs). As previously mentioned, no adjustment is provided. As regards lubrication, the only attention needed is re-packing of the bearings with grease during a complete overhaul.

To Remove Rear Wheel (Models With Rigid Frames or Plunger Type Rear Springing). To facilitate removal of the quickly-detachable rear

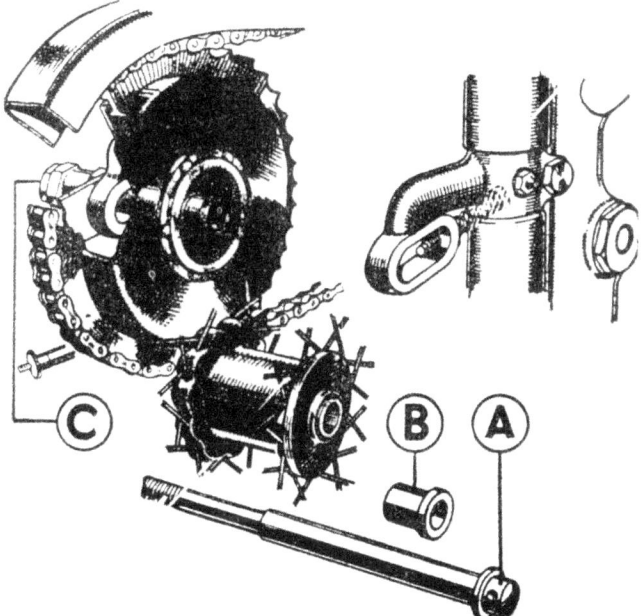

FIG. 71. REAR WHEEL REMOVAL
Models with plunger type rear springing

wheel the tail of the mudguard is hinged. Disconnect the tail lamp wire at the coupling provided; also loosen the nuts at the fixing stays.

Referring to Figs. 71, 72, remove the near-side outer spindle nut (C). On spring frame models do not touch the large sleeve nut located behind nut (C). This nut needs to be slackened only during the adjustment of the secondary chain (*see* page 114). Remove the wheel spindle by inserting a suitable tommy-bar into the head of the spindle at (A) and turning *anti-clockwise*. Remove the distance piece (B). As the spindle is withdrawn it will probably fall out. Now withdraw the rear wheel. Pull it towards the off-side of the motor-cycle into the space left by the removal of the distance piece (*B*). This disengages the coupling splines on the hub from the brake drum.

To Remove Front Wheel (1958–62 Models). Referring to Fig. 73, to remove the front wheel (all models), first disconnect the brake cable. Then remove the four bolts (*A*) and pull the front wheel away from the telescopic front forks. Note that when replacing the front wheel the brake anchorage

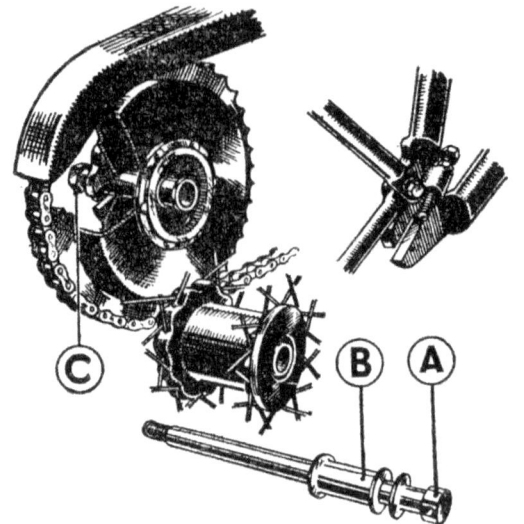

FIG. 72. REAR WHEEL REMOVAL
Rigid frame models.

peg on the off-side fork leg must engage correctly in the slot in the brake cover plate.

To Remove Front Wheel (1955–7 Full-width Hub). Referring to Fig. 74, to remove the front wheel, first remove the nut (*C*) from the brake coverplate; also disconnect the brake cable. Now slacken the pinch-bolt (*A*) and remove the nut (*E*) on the opposite side. It has a normal right-hand thread. Then with a tommy-bar inserted into the hole on the head of the wheel spindle (*B*), pull the spindle out. When doing this, support the weight of the front wheel. As the spindle emerges, pull the wheel away from the off-side fork leg and remove it. Be careful not to allow the wheel to fall on the bush projecting from the brake-drum side. Although the bush is pressed in, a sharp blow on it may force the bush back into the hub. The remedy in this case is to retrieve and re-position the bush by means of the front-wheel spindle.

When replacing the front wheel, see that all nuts and the pinch-bolt (*A*) are firmly re-tightened. *Before* tightening the pinch-bolt and *after* tightening the spindle nut (*E*), it is essential to depress the forks once or twice to enable the near-side fork end to position itself on the spindle shank. Failure

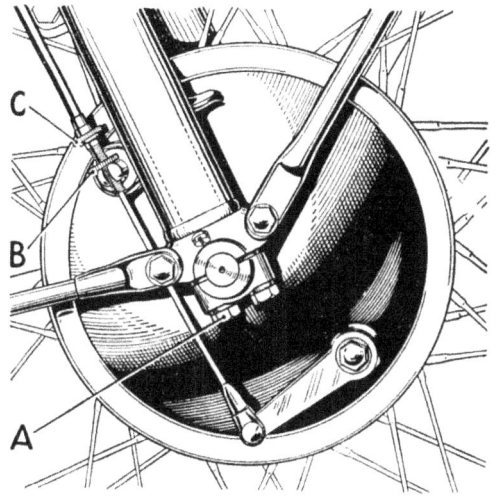

FIG. 73. FRONT WHEEL REMOVAL AND BRAKE ADJUSTMENT (1958-9)

A. Nuts securing hub spindle
B. Lock-nut for *C*
C. Front brake adjuster (on handlebars, 1960-2)

to observe this precaution may cause the near-side fork leg to be clamped out of position, thereby preventing the forks from functioning correctly.

To Remove Front Wheel (Pre-1955, 8-in. Brake). On pre-1955 machines (A7 Star Twin and A10 Golden Flash) having the front brake arrangement shown in Fig. 75, first remove the nut (*C*) on the cover plate, and loosen the nuts (*D*) at the opposite end of the brake anchor-strap. Uncouple the brake cable, first at the lever (*E*) on the brake cover-plate, and then at the cable stop (*F*). Loosen the pinch-bolt (*A*) which is fitted only to the near-side fork leg and locks the wheel spindle. Now unscrew the wheel spindle after inserting a tommy-bar through the spindle head at (*B*) and turning the spindle (L.H. thread) *clockwise*. Withdraw the wheel spindle from the near-side while supporting the front wheel. The latter is now free to be removed from the telescopic front forks.

After removing the front wheel, avoid allowing the weight of the wheel to contact the bush which projects from the brake side of the hub. The bush is pressed in but nevertheless, if subjected to a sharp blow, may fall inside the cover plate. This would, of course, entail removal of the cover plate to retrieve and locate the bush.

To Remove Front Wheel (Pre-1954, 7-in. Brake). To remove the front wheel from A7 models provided with a 7-in. diameter brake drum (the

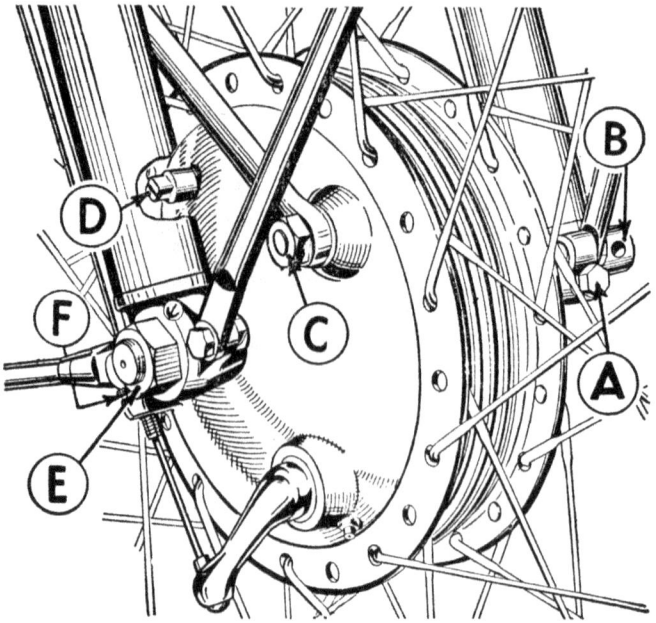

FIG. 74. FRONT WHEEL REMOVAL
1955-7 full-width hub.

method of securing the front wheel is shown in Fig. 76), uncouple the cable, first at the lever on the brake anchor-plate, and then unscrew the cable adjuster from the stop.

Next, referring to Fig. 76, which shows the off-side of the wheel assembly, slacken the pinch-bolt (A), situated at the front of the near-side fork leg. Unscrew the wheel spindle with a tommy bar inserted through the hole (B) in the spindle end. Turn the tommy bar *clockwise*, as the spindle has a *left-hand thread*. Withdraw the spindle from the near side while supporting the weight of the wheel with one hand, and slide the distance bush

GENERAL MAINTENANCE

(*C*), in the fork end, outwards to its full extent. The front wheel should then come away.

After replacing the wheel spindle, *before* tightening the pinch-bolt (*A*) depress the forks several times. This permits the near-side fork leg to position itself properly on the distance bush. Unless this is done, the near-side fork leg may not align itself properly and the forks may not function satisfactorily. Be sure to re-tighten the pinch-bolt (*A*) firmly. On the A7 model see that the peg on the brake cover-plate fits properly into its socket on the fork leg, otherwise the brake will fail to operate. On the A7 Star Twin and A10 models replace the brake anchor-strap carefully.

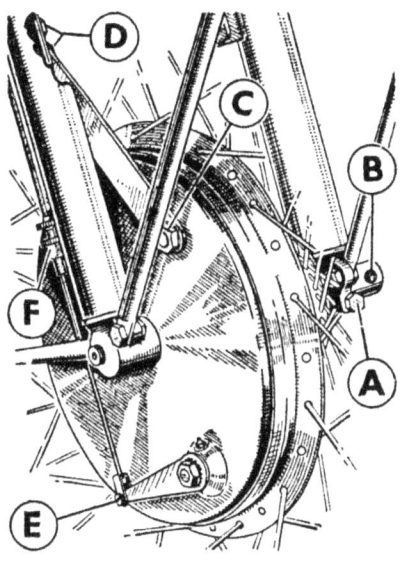

Fig. 75. Front Wheel Removal
Pre-1955 8 in. brake.

Checking Wheel Alignment. It is advisable to check wheel alignment after the tension of the secondary chain is checked. If the wheels were previously in true alignment and the chain tension adjusters have both been moved to the same extent, then the wheel alignment should, of course, remain correct.

Check wheel alignment by glancing along the line of both wheels when the front wheel is set straight, or by means of a long straight-edge placed along the sides of both tyres, but remember that the difference in tyre sizes must be taken into account where this exists. Apply the straight-edge at a point immediately below the silencer and keep it in a horizontal position. With the front wheel set parallel with the rear one, the straight-edge should contact the front and rear tyres (provided they are of the same size) at four points. A taut length of string can be used as an alternative to a straight-edge. One end can be attached to a suitable anchorage post. *See* also page 130.

Front Brake Adjustment. The length of the brake cable can be altered at its lower end, the adjuster being a knurled thumb nut on the cable stop. On 1960–2 models a knurled screw adjuster is provided on the handlebar lever.

Rear Brake Adjustment. This brake has finger adjustment at the end of the brake rod (*see* Fig. 77) or a screwed sleeve and lock-nut mounted

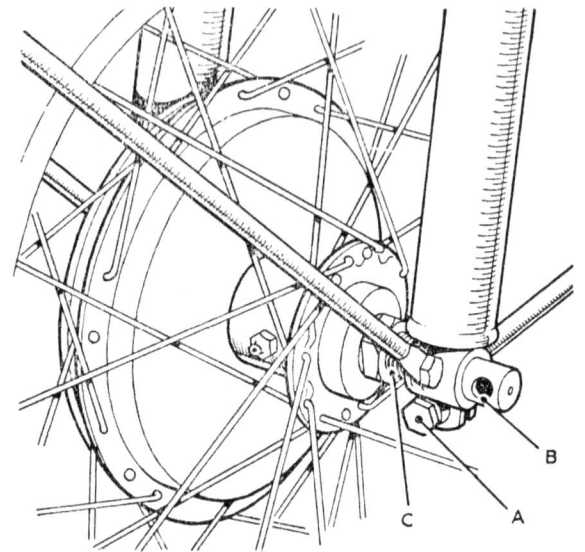

Fig. 76. Front Wheel Removal
Pre-1954 7 in. brake.

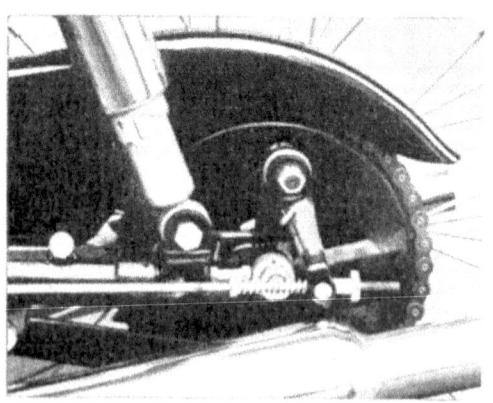

Fig. 77. Rear Brake Adjustment

GENERAL MAINTENANCE

on the anchor plate when a chain-case is fitted. Be careful not to adjust either front or rear brake too closely. An instantaneous powerful brake action is undesirable, and friction caused through too close an adjustment will obviously have an adverse effect on the performance of the machine. Friction will also generate heat and may cause the grease in the hubs to melt and reach the brake linings. This causes general inefficiency and can be dangerous.

Brake Shoe Removal (1958–62 Models). Slacken the brake shoe adjuster fully, and remove the brake plate from the wheel. Then grasp the shoes firmly, pulling outwards, thus enabling the shoes to clear the fulcrums and lift. The shoes can be replaced by the reverse procedure. Hook the spring on to the shoes and place the ends of the shoes in position on the fulcrum pins, pushing the shoes outwards until the springs pull them into their correct position. Note that the brake shoe springs are quite strong, and care must be taken to avoid trapping the fingers. (*See* also page 129.)

Brake Shoe Linings. Note that complete relined brake shoes are available through the B.S.A. exchange-replacement service. This operates in the British Isles only. On the Super Rocket model the brake shoes are of the floating type and the linings are not symmetrical with the shoes. It is therefore important to see that they are properly fitted. The shoes are marked "L" and "T" for "leading" and "trailing," the leading shoe being opened by the cam in the direction of wheel rotation.

Steering Head Adjustment. Test the steering head for play occasionally and make sure that it rotates freely. Support the crankcase on a box so that the front wheel is clear of the ground (*see* Fig. 78). Then grasp the front fork legs and attempt to push them backwards and forwards. If you detect any play, make an adjustment.

Referring to Fig. 79, unscrew the steering damper and remove the chromium-plated top cap (*B*). Prior to removing the steering damper knob with stem, withdraw the split pin (where fitted) at its lower end. Slacken the clamping nut (*C*) and then, after slackening the fork-yoke pinch bolts (*D*), tighten down the sleeve (*E*) until the steering adjustment is correct. Hold the handlebars lightly and move them round slowly. The steering should be free, and the forks must rotate smoothly. If the movement is "lumpy" this indicates that the adjustment is too tight, and this may cause the ball races to become damaged. When the adjustment is correct tighten the clamping nut (*C*), replace the cap (*B*) and the steering damper. Also tighten the fork-yoke pinch bolts (*D*).

Dismantling of the Forks. Complete dismantling of the forks should not be attempted without two special tools, Part Nos. 61–3350 and 61–3005.

Remove the front wheel and front mudguard. Remove the cap *A*

(Fig. 79) and screw tool 61-3350 into the thread in the top of the main fork shaft. Slacken the pinch-bolt *D*. By striking the top of the tool smartly with a hammer the fork shaft will be freed from its taper in the top fork yoke and the complete fork leg can be pulled out from the bottom of the fork. Repeat the operation for the other leg. Note that the smaller of the two fine threads on the extractor tool is used for dismantling the forks on

FIG. 78. TESTING FOR PLAY IN STEERING HEAD

another model and will therefore not be used. In an emergency the chromium plated cap can be used in place of the extractor, but it is likely to be damaged.

Hold the bottom of the sliding member by gripping the wheel spindle lug in a soft-jawed vice and lift off the spring (*see* Fig. 80). The special unscrewing tool 61-3005 consists of a tubular member with two dogs which engage in slots cut in the bottom spring seating. Engage the tool and unscrew the chromium-plated spring shroud. The oil seal is contained in the bottom of the spring shroud and can be pressed out with a drift passed through the two slots. Do not remove the oil seal unless it requires replacing.

The top bearing of the sliding member is now retained only by a circlip which can be prised out with a suitable sharp tool. Note that a number of shims may be fitted between the circlip and the top of the bearing. These

GENERAL MAINTENANCE

must be replaced during re-assembly and if any movement of the bearing is still apparent when the circlip has been replaced, additional shims should be used. If there is any play at this point a clicking noise may be heard when the forks are operating.

With the circlip removed the complete fork shaft and bushes can be withdrawn from the sliding member.

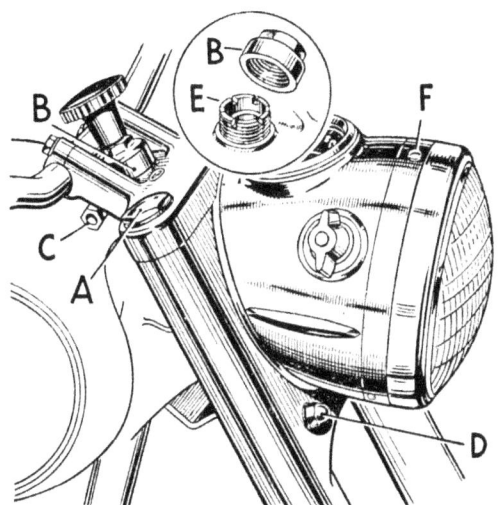

FIG. 79. SHOWING STEERING HEAD DETAILS

The bottom nut retaining the bronze bushes can be unscrewed with the fork shaft gripped in a soft jawed vice to prevent it turning.

To remove the two yokes and the steering stem from the frame, undo the clamping nut *C* (Fig. 79). Remove the steering damper knob and the cap *B*. Unscrew the sleeve *E* until it comes free, and then lift off the top yoke. Take care that the balls from the head bearings are not lost when the head is loosened.

The bearing cups which remain in the head can be withdrawn with the aid of a screwed extractor, Part No. 61-3063. This should be screwed firmly into the threaded centre of the cup; then extractor and cup can be driven out from the opposite end with a suitable punch. The races must be replaced if they show any signs of pitting, as damaged head races will affect the steering.

If the forks have been damaged in any way the shafts must be checked to ensure that they are perfectly straight. It is also possible to twist the yokes so that even if new shafts are used they will not be in line. This can be checked by clamping the new shafts into the lower yoke; then check that the shafts are not twisted by placing them on a surface plate or on two parallel straight-edges. Also check that when the top yoke is slid down the head-stem sleeve on to the shafts, the tapers meet squarely. If they are only lightly twisted it is possible to reset the yokes, but replacements are preferable.

Re-assembly is carried out in the reverse order to dismantling. Make sure the oil seal lip is facing downwards. Before screwing down the oil seal holder, pass one turn of medium twine round the undercut at the base of the thread to provide an additional seal. When

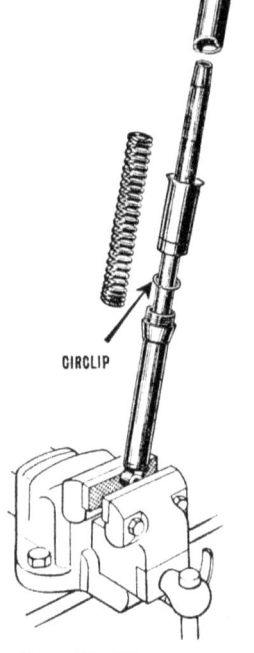

FIG. 80. DISMANTLING THE FRONT FORKS

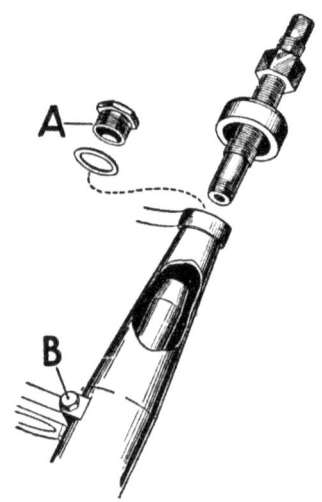

FIG. 81. SOME FORK ASSEMBLY DETAILS

replacing the legs pass the main fork shaft up through the bottom yoke as far as it will go; then pass the tool 61-3350 down through the top yoke and screw it into the top of the shaft (Fig. 81). Do up the nut on the tool to pull the shaft up into the top yoke. Tighten the clamp in the bottom yoke while the tool is removed and the top plug replaced. Slacken the lower clamp, tighten the top plug firmly, then do up the clamp again. Alternatively, in an emergency, a suitable sized length of wood, cut to a taper at the end, can be screwed into the top of the shaft.

Rear Suspension. The two S.A.-type units comprise a telescopic damper unit and a totally enclosed coil spring. The pressure on the spring can be varied by means of a three-position cam adjuster (*see* Fig. 82) at the lower end of the unit. The springs can therefore be adjusted to suit the load conditions or nature of the ground. For rotating the cam ring a "C" spanner is provided in the tool kit.

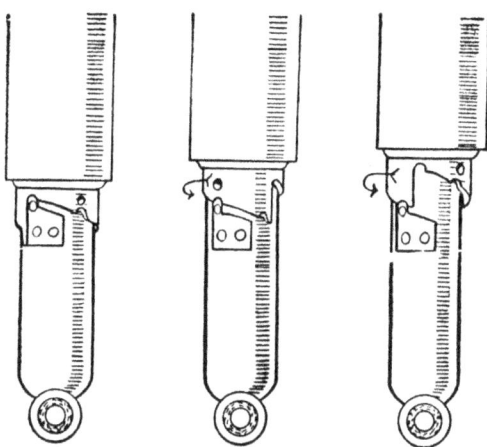

FIG. 82. THE REAR SUSPENSION ADJUSTMENTS
Showing three adjustments on "swinging arm" models

The hydraulic dampers require no attention whatever. They are sealed during manufacture and must be replaced if they suffer damage or become ineffective. The complete suspension units can be removed from the frame after detaching the two pivot bolts. The top spring housing is retained by two collets and the spring must be compressed before they can be removed. The assistance of a second person in some instances is necessary to compress the spring.

Tyre Pressures. For solo riding 18 lb and 20 lb per sq in. are recommended for the front and rear tyres respectively on most recent A7 and A10 models. Where a pillion passenger is carried the pressure of the rear tyre can be increased to about 28 lb per sq in.; a sidecar tyre pressure should always be about 20 lb per sq in.

Brake Shoe Removal (1955–7). Remove the brake plate from the wheel and remove the split pin locking the nut on the brake cam spindle. Remove the nut and washer and take out the spindle. Slacken the brake shoe adjuster and lift out both brake shoes.

Wheel Alignment (Sidecar Outfits). Checking wheel alignment on a solo model is referred to on page 123. In the case of a sidecar outfit first check the alignment of the motor-cycle front and rear wheels as described on that page. Then, with your sidecar outfit on a smooth, level surface, position (about 4 in. above the ground) the previously-mentioned straight-edge alongside the rear tyre of the motor-cycle, and another similar straight-edge alongside the sidecar tyre as shown in Fig. 83. Check the difference between distances A and B. The sidecar wheel "toe-in" is

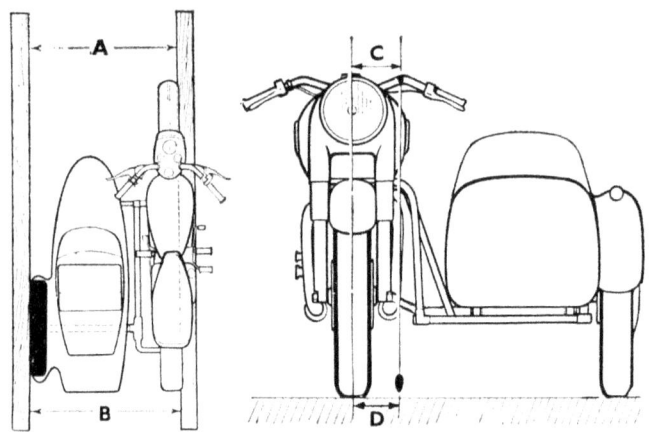

FIG. 83. SHOWING (LEFT) WHEEL ALIGNMENT CHECK FOR SIDECAR "TOE-IN," AND (RIGHT) DIMENSIONAL CHECK FOR MOTOR-CYCLE "LEAN-OUT"

The "toe-in" is, of course, the difference between distances A and B; the "lean-out" is the difference between distances C and D. For checking the former, two straight-edges are required, and for checking the latter a plumb line is needed

(*B.S.A. Motor Cycles Ltd.*)

correct if A is $\frac{3}{8}$ in.–$\frac{3}{4}$ in. less than B, the precise dimension depending on the type and make of sidecar fitted. Should the "toe-in" be found to be incorrect, adjust the sidecar fittings as required in accordance with the maker's instructions.

The B.S.A. A7 or A10 model itself should lean out about 1 in. out of the vertical, towards the *off-side*. Check this alignment by attaching a plumb line to the near-side of the handlebars and taking measurements between the plumb line and the vertical centre-line of the front wheel. Distance C should be 1 in. more than distance D; if necessary, adjust the telescopic arms of the sidecar chassis as required. When attaching a sidecar, checking "toe-in" and attending to sidecar maintenance (*see* page 74), follow exactly the sidecar maker's instructions.

When Attaching a Sidecar. Note that stronger telescopic front-fork springs are usually required for a sidecar outfit than for a solo model. If you attach a sidecar to a B.S.A. twin bought for solo use, take your motor-cycle to a B.S.A. dealer and ask him to fit heavy-duty springs of suitable type. Do not attempt to fit these springs yourself.

Index

Accessory firms, 75
Air cleaner, 36-8
Alignment, wheel, 123, 130
Amal carburettor—
  maintenance, 30-5
  working of, 19-23
Ammeter, 7, 43
Anti-syphon valve—
  sticking, 65
Automatic ignition-advance, 87

Battery—
  care of, 44-9
  connexions, 49
  disconnecting, 39, 55
Bores—
  cylinder block, 99
Brake—
  adjustment, 123
  lubrication, 73-4
  pedal, 73
  shoes, 122-4
  usage, 14
Bulb renewal, 51-4

C. & W. Air cleaner, 37
Cables—
  high-tension, 87
Carbon deposits—
  removing, 95
Carburettor—
  adjustment, 25-30
  flange, 34
  maintenance, 30-5
  on fire, 12
  settings, 26
  working of, 19-23
Chain—
  adjustment, 108, 114
  lubrication, 67, 70
  stretch, 117
Cleaning—
  carburettor, 32
  chromium surfaces, 78

Cleaning (contd.)—
  contact-breaker, 83
  enamelled parts, 78
  engine and gearbox, 78
  filters, 63
  headlamps, 54
  sparking plugs, 80-3
Clutch—
  dismantling, 111-14
  plates—
    sticking, 12
  spring pressure, 109
Commutator, 40, 41
Compensated voltage control, 42
Control cables, 73
Controls, 10, 47
Crankcase—
  draining, 62
Cross-over shaft—
  brake, 73
Cylinder—
  block—
    removing, 99
    replacing, 103
  head—
    removal, 91-3
    replacing, 103-5

Decarbonizing, 90-106
Draining gearbox, 70
Driving licence, 1
Dry sump lubrication, 61
Dualseat, removing, 44
Dynamo—
  lubrication, 66
  maintenance, 39-42
  removal, 67

Enamelled parts—
  cleaning, 78
Engine—
  controls, 4
  number, 1
  shaft shock-absorber, 71
  suitable oils, 59

INDEX

FILTERS—
 cleaning, 63
Float chamber, 34
Flooding—
 causes of, 31
Focusing headlamps, 50-1
Footrest adjustment, 3
Frame number, 1
Front forks, 72, 125-8
Fuel replenishment, 8

GAP—
 contact-breaker, 84
 sparking plug, 80
 valve stem, 88-90
Gear changing, 12-14
Gearbox—
 draining, 70
 lubrication, 68
 repairs, 117
Greases—
 recommended, 67
Grinding-in valves, 96
Gudgeon-pin removal, 102

HANDLEBAR controls—
 lubricating, 73
Headlamp—
 maintenance, 54
 position, 49
High-tension—
 cables, 87
 pickups, 87
Hill climbing, 15
Horn, 54
Hub lubrication, 71
Hydrometer, 47

IGNITION—
 lever, 4
 timing, 84-6
Ignition-advance unit—
 automatic, 87
Induction bias, 29

JET—
 block, 34
 main, 22
 needle clip, 34
  position, 28
  wear, 35

LAMP failure, 58
Lighting switch positions, 49
Lubrication—
 brake, 73-4
 chart, 69
 dynamo, 66
 engine, 59-66
 front forks, 72
 gearbox, 68
 handlebar controls, 73
 magneto, 66
 primary chain, 67
 rear suspension, 73
 saddle-nose bolt, 73
 secondary chain, 70
 sidecar chassis, 74
 stands, 74
 steering head, 71
 wheel bearings, 71
Lucas battery filler, 45

MAGNETO lubrication, 66
Maintenance—
 items for, 76
Mechanical breather—
 crankcase, 66
"Monobloc" carburettor, 22
Motor-cycle controls, 5

NEUTRAL, 14
Nuts—
 tightness of, 79

OIL—
 breather tower, 65
 circulation—
  checking, 60
 pressure-control valve, 64
 tank—
  draining, 62
  pressure-release pipe, 65
  replenishing, 9, 59
Overhead rockers—
 removing, 98

PARKING, 15
Petrol—
 consumption—
  excessive, 30
 tank removal, 91

Pick-up, high-tension, 87
Pilot jet—
  adjustment, 26
  obstructed, 28
Piston—
  removal, 101–3
  rings, 100
Pistons—
  replacing, 103
Plunger-type rear springing, 73
Preliminaries, 1, 18
Primary chain—
  adjustment, 108–9
  lubrication, 67
Prop stand, 8

REAR suspension, 128
Repair work—
  tools for, 77
Riding—
  hints, 18
  position, 2
Rocker-box and cylinder head
    removal, 91–3
Running-in, 17, 79

SADDLE-NOSE bolt—
  lubricating, 73
Secondary chain—
  adjustment, 114–16
  enclosure, 118
  lubrication, 70
Sidecar, 74, 130
Slow-running—
  indifferent, 28
  mixture, 25–7, 29–30
Spares and repairs, 75
Sparking plugs, 79–83
Specific gravity—
  electrolyte, 47
Speedometer, 7
Speedometer drive, 73
Stands, 8, 74

Starting—
  trouble, 11
  up, 10
Steering—
  damper, 7
  head—
    adjustment, 125
    lubrication, 71
Stopping procedure, 14
Storage—
  battery, 49
"Swinging arm" rear suspension, 73

"TEKALL," 78
Terminals—
  dynamo, 42
Theft—
  preventing, 15
Throttle valve, 34
Timing—
  ignition, 84–6
  valve, 106–8
Tool kit, 76
Topping-up battery, 44
Twin carburettor—
  tuning, 29
Tyre pressures, 129

VALVE—
  clearances, 88–90
  guides—
    worn, 97
  springs, 96
  timing, 106–8
Valves—
  assembling, 98
  grinding-in, 96
  removing, 93–5
Vokes air cleaner, 36

WHEEL—
  alignment, 123, 130
  removal, 117–23
Wiring diagrams, 56–7

OTHER CLASSIC MOTORCYCLE MANUALS CURRENTLY AVAILABLE

ARIEL WORKSHOP MANUAL 1933-1951:
All single, twin & 4 cylinder models

ARIEL (BOOK OF) MAINTENANCE & REPAIR MANUAL 1932-1939:
LF3, LF4, LG, NF3, NF4, NG, OG, VA, VA3, VA4, VB, VF3, VF4, VG, Red Hunter LH, NH, OH, VH & Square Four 4F, 4G, 4H

BMW FACTORY WORKSHOP MANUAL R27, R28:
English, German, French and Spanish text

BMW FACTORY WORKSHOP MANUAL R50, R50S, R60, R69S:
Also includes a supplement for the USA models: R50US, R60US, R69US.
English, German, French and Spanish text

BSA (BOOK OF) MAINTENANCE & REPAIR 1936-1939:
All Pre-War single & twin cylinder SV & OHV models through 1939
150cc, 250cc, 350cc, 500cc, 600cc, 750cc & 1,000cc

DUCATI OHC FACTORY WORKSHOP MANUAL:
160 Junior Monza, 250 Monza, 250 GT, 250 Mark 3, 250 Mach 1, 250 SCR & 350 Sebring

HONDA 250 & 305cc FACTORY WORKSHOP MANUAL:
C.72 C.77 CS.72, CS.77, CB.72, CB.77 [HAWK]

HONDA 125 & 150cc FACTORY WORKSHOP MANUAL:
C.92, CS.92, CB.92, C.95 & CA.95

HONDA 50cc FACTORY WORKSHOP MANUAL: C.100

HONDA 50cc FACTORY WORKSHOP MANUAL: C.110

HONDA (BOOK OF) MAINTENANCE & REPAIR 1960-1966:
50cc C.100, C.102, C.110 & C.114 ~ 125cc C.92 & CB.92
250cc C.72 & CB.72 ~ 305cc CB.77

LAMBRETTA (BOOK OF) MAINTENANCE & REPAIR:
125 & 150cc, all models up to 1958, except model "48".

NORTON FACTORY TWIN CYLINDER WORKSHOP MANUAL 1957-1970: *Lightweight Twins:* 250cc Jubilee, 350cc Navigator and 400cc Electra and the *Heavyweight Twins:* Model 77, 88, 88SS, 99, 99SS, Sports Special, Manxman, Mercury, Atlas, G15, P11, N15, Ranger (P11A).

NORTON (BOOK OF) MAINTENANCE & REPAIR 1932-1939:
All Pre-War SV, OHV and OHC models: 16H, 16I, 18, 19, 20, 50, 55, ES2, CJ, CSI, International 30 & 40

SUZUKI 200 & 250cc FACTORY WORKSHOP MANUAL:
250cc T20 [X-6 Hustler] ~ 200cc T200 [X-5 Invader & Sting Ray Scrambler]

SUZUKI 250cc FACTORY WORKSHOP MANUAL: 250cc ~ T10

TRIUMPH (BOOK OF) MAINTENANCE & REPAIR 1935-1939:
All Pre-War single & twin cylinder models: L2/1, 2/1, 2/5, 3/1, 3/2, 3/5, 5/1, 5/2, 5/3, 5/4, 5/5, 5/10, 6/1, Tiger 70, 80, 90 & 2H. Tiger 70C, 3S & 3H, Tiger 80C & 5H, Tiger 90C, 6S, 2HC & 3SC, 5T Speed Twin & 5S and T100 Tiger 100

TRIUMPH 1937-1951 WORKSHOP MANUAL (A. St. J. Masters):
Covers rigid frame and sprung hub single cylinder SV & OHV and twin cylinder OHV pre-war, military, and post-war models

TRIUMPH 1945-1955 FACTORY WORKSHOP MANUAL NO.11:
Covers pre-unit, twin-cylinder rigid frame, sprung hub, swing-arm and 350cc, 500cc & 650cc.

VESPA (BOOK OF) MAINTENANCE & REPAIR 1946-1959:
All 125cc & 150cc models including 42/L2 & Gran Sport

VINCENT WORKSHOP MANUAL 1935-1955:
All Series A, B & C Models

COMING SOON IN THIS SAME SERIES:

BRIDGESTONE FACTORY WORKSHOP MANUAL: 50 Sport, 60 Sport, 90 De Luxe, 90 Trail, 90 Mountain, 90 Sport, 175 Dual Twin & Hurricane

BRITISH MILITARY MAINTENANCE & REPAIR MANUAL:
Service & Repair data for all British WD motorcycles

BRITISH MOTORCYCLE ENGINES: AJS, Ariel, BSA, Excelsior, JAP, Norton, Royal Enfield, Rudge, Scott, Sunbeam, Triumph, Velocette, Villiers & Vincent ~ a compilation of 1950's articles from *The Motor Cycle* dealing with engine design.

CEZETTA 175cc MODEL 501 MANUAL & PARTS BOOK

VILLIERS ENGINE WORKSHOP MANUAL:
All Villiers engines and ancillaries through 1947

PLEASE CHECK OUR WEBSITE FOR AVAILABILITY
~ WWW.VELOCEPRESS.COM ~

www.ingramcontent.com/pod-product-compliance
Lightning Source LLC
Chambersburg PA
CBHW070553170426
43201CB00012B/1829